Barcelona

COLLINS

Glasgow & London

First published 1990
Copyright © William Collins Sons & Company Limited
Published by William Collins Sons & Company Limited
Printed in Hong Kong
ISBN 0 00 435771-X

HOW TO USE THIS BOOK

Your Collins Traveller Guide will help you find your way around your chosen destination quickly and easily. It is colour-coded for easy reference:

The blue-coded 'topic' section answers the question 'I would like to see or do something; where do I go and what do I see when I get there?' A simple, clear layout provides an alphabetical list of activities and events, offers you a selection of each, tells you how to get there, what it will cost, when it is open and what to expect. Each topic in the list has its own simplified map, showing the position of each item and the nearest landmark or transport access, for instant orientation. Whether your interest is Architecture or Sport you can find all the information you need quickly and simply. Where major resorts within an area require in-depth treatment, they follow the main topics section in alphabetical order.

The red-coded section is a lively and informative gazetteer. In one alphabetical list you can find essential facts about the main places and cultural items - 'What is La Bastille?', 'Who was Michelangelo?' - as well as practical and invaluable travel information. It covers everything you need to know to help you enjoy yourself and get the most out of your time away, from Accommodation through Babysitters, Car Hire, Food, Health, Money, Newspapers, Taxis and Telephones to Zoos.

Cross-references: Type in small capitals - CHURCHES - tells you that more information on an item is available within the topic on churches. A-Z in bold - A-Z - tells you that more information is available on an item within the gazetteer. Simply look under the appropriate heading. A name in bold - Holy Cathedral - also tells you that more information on an item is available in the gazetteer under that particular heading.

Packed full of information and easy to use - you'll always know where you are with your Collins Traveller Guide!

La Rambla

Castillian Spanish is the official language of Spain but in Barcelona Catalan, a separate language, is given equal ranking. Although Castillian and, increasingly, English are understood you will find that some signs are in Catalan only.

Photographs by **Jan Kruse**

INTRODUCTION

Barcelona is Spain's second biggest city and capital of Catalunya, the country's wealthiest region. More significantly, Barcelona has for eleven centuries been the capital of the Catalan people who, by reason of geography and historical experience, have a language and cultural identity distinct from that of their Spanish cousins. In the past, while the rest of Spain raised barriers against foreign influences, cosmopolitan ideas soaked into the absorbent tissue of Catalan society, enriching it economically and culturally. During its medieval golden age, Barcelona reigned as queen among Mediterranean port-cities. With an unmatched verve it is striving to do so again. Barcelona, *Mes Que Mai*, Barcelona, 'More than Ever', bright banners everywhere proclaim. It is a slogan, in Catalan, given meaning by the commitment to progress of its civic bodies and the supportive enthusiasm of Barcelonans. People who believe they live in Europe's most vibrantly progressive city are proud to show it off. Twice within the last hundred years Barcelona has hosted Universal Exhibitions which fostered fresh artistic directions and renewed the city's fabric. As venue for the Summer Olympics of 1992, Barcelona is once again assured of the world's attention.

There is much to see, most of it so captivating that enthralled admirers cannot resist visiting the city time after time. There are blemishes too, but no conurbation with a population of over three million is without those. The Collins Traveller introduces the best that Barcelona offers - from the stunning architecture of its rich cultural heritage to the vibrant night-scenes of its heady lifestyle.

Gothic and Gaudí, architectural style and architectural genius, the city is hugely endowed with a legacy from both. The evocative Barri Gotic is a maze of alleys and grand buildings built upon Roman Barcino. Antoni Gaudí's weird and wonderful creations are mostly in the Eixample, the grid-form 19thC extension of the city, where buildings of many other *modernista* architects also show the inspiration of Catalan history and craft traditions in ceramics, glass and wrought iron. In our time, Barcelonans, like Ricardo Bofill, and leading architects from around the world are again enhancing the cityscape.

Where a mild Mediterranean climate predominates, life takes place outdoors as much as indoors. In Barcelona they enjoy some of Europe's most delightful avenues, squares and gardens which are being further

9

endowed with new public art. By day and night, buzzing La Rambla is surely the world's most animated street. Passeig de Gracia, by contrast, is a grand avenue of quiet elegance. The new Moll de la Fusta is one of the projects by which the city is again being opened to its sea. Another is the Olympic Village. Montjuïc, a green, landscaped hill, rises gently above the city and is packed with places of interest - cultural, sports and entertainment.

Outstanding among Barcelona's many and varied museums is the Museu d'Art de Catalunya with its exceptional collection of Romanesque and Gothic works. Art of the famous Catalan surrealist, Joan Miró, is shown at the Fundacio Miró, a lively centre of contemporary culture. There are many more such centres, theatres, galleries, cafes with music or shows, giving visitors easy access to Barcelona's vibrant cultural life, past and present. Music-lovers can enjoy a double treat, very varied programmes of fine music presented in the Palau de la Musica Catalana, by any judgement surely the world's most fascinating venue.

Barcelona is a new hotspot on the international fashion and design scene. Its PoMo boutiques, elegant shops and their fashion-flaunting customers are visual proof. Besides clothing, there's the best from Spain's newly acclaimed designers in jewellery, housewares, lighting, furniture and decorative pieces. But anyone in search of old craft goods, antique pieces or just the zany also has plenty of choice. A number of malls, like Bulevard Rosa, offer convenient one-stop shopping. Other cities destroy their central food markets, Barcelona raises its bustling La Boqueria to the status of an urban treasure.

Eating and drinking well is a Catalan habit and Barcelona caters nobly for every taste and budget. Bars, quick-bites and take-aways are everywhere. Traditional, atmospheric places serve hearty, inexpensive meals based on the best local produce. The beachside area of Barceloneta is awash with eateries serving the freshest of seafoods. Pricier are smart, uptown restaurants where innovative chefs preserve the taste and texture of fresh harvests from land and sea, presenting modern Mediterranean cuisine at its best.

And as for its nightlife, well, action or entertainment, visitors will find whatever they seek. From the low-life and raunchiness of a big port-city to huge, bare discos where beautiful people are the decor. The Barri Xines has for long been Barcelona's notorious red-light district. Some places stage shows which are luridly pornographic, others have sophisticated cabarets or good flamenco. Gentility and nostalgia rule in the city's dance halls. *Xampanyerias* which serve the very drinkable Catalan cava are elegant pre-dinner venues. After dinner, the in-scene moves to high-fashion bars whose music, video and light presentations compete with the best of the discos, next stop of the most energetic pleasure seekers.

By day, walking its streets is the best way to discover any city and the Collins Traveller presents three suggested daytime **WALKS** which take in many of the sightseeing highlights. See also **CITY DISTRICTS**. Using the bus network is also a good idea. Taxis are plentiful and relatively inexpensive. The metro is handy within the central areas, especially for getting around quickly during rush hours. City tours by coach are a fast and easy way of getting orientated. Driving is not recommended for newcomers to the city.

Cablecars ride high above the harbour while small excursion boats ply across it. A trip by tram and funicular to the top of Tibidabo hill is a favourite family-fun treat. Catalunya is a beautiful and most fascinating region so there are a host of places beyond the city, inland or along the coast, which its longer-stay visitors can easily discover on organised tours or independently. The mountain and monastery of Montserrat, spiritual centre of the Catalans, attracts the biggest numbers. By contrast, there's the wine town of Sant Sadurni and, on the Costa Daurada, Sitges ranks among Spain's most delightful and smartest seaside resorts. Barcelona beckons!

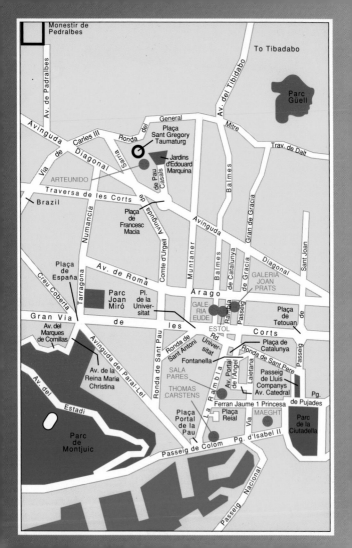

ARTEUNIDO
Plaça Sant Gregori Taumaturg 1.
Bus 66 from Plaça Catalunya.
Changing shows of contemporary artists, many local. One of several good galleries in the area.

ESTOL
Consell de Cent 286.
M Passeig de Gràcia.
Original paintings, sculptures and ceramics. Mostly little-known artists.

GALERIA EUDE
Consell de Cent 278.
M Passeig de Gràcia.
One of the many galleries on this block between Rambla de Catalunya and Balmes. Known for mounting good visiting exhibitions.

GALERIA JOAN PRATS
Rambla de Catalunya 54.
M Passeig de Gràcia.
Contemporary works are well-exhibited in a series of small rooms.

THOMAS CARSTENS
Josep Ansel Clave 4.
M Drassanes.
A place to see way-out work of the vanguardistas.

MAEGHT
Montcada 25.
M Jaume I.
Displays of contemporary creations housed in a lovely old palace.

SALA PARES
Petritxol 5.
M Liceu.
Features Catalan painters but there are also changing exhibitions.

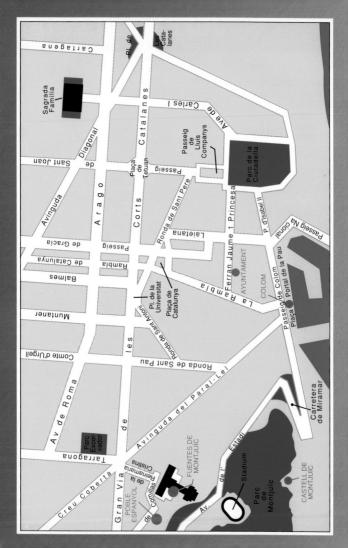

AYUNTAMENT Plaça Sant Jaume.

M Jaume I.

The City Hall. Neo-classical front added in 1840s to a medieval building. Old entrance and Gothic facade on Carrer de la Ciutat. Entrance patio has work by leading Catalan sculptors. In the Saló de las Crònicas there's an epic mural by Josep Sert (1928).

POBLE ESPANYOL Avinguda de Marques de Comillas.

•0900-1900. M Plaça Espanya then Bus 61.

Copies of buildings, facades and plazas from among the whole of Spain's rich architectural heritage are grouped together by region in this mock village. There is also a museum of traditional arts and industries, craft shops, restaurants.

CASTELL DE MONTJUIC

•0900-1900. Museum 1000-1400 and 1600-1900.

M Plaça Espanya, then Bus 61 or 201, then Funicular or Teleferic.

Sprawling fortifications. Good views over port. A museum chronicles the place's unhappy history since 1640. Also has models of other Catalan castles and the Frederic Mares collection of weapons.

FUENTES DE MONTJUÏC

Below Palau Nacional.

Performances.•Summer: 2100-2400 Thurs., Sat., Sun. and holidays, 2200-2300 with music.•Winter: one hour earlier and not Thurs.

M Plaça Espanya.

Searchlights from the Palau Nacional pierce the sky. Extensive fountains, coloured lights and music combine in one hour display.

COLOM (Columbus) Plaça Portal de la Pau.

Lift to viewing platform: •0930-1330 and 1630-1830. M Drassanes.

Erected for the 1888 Exhibition.

A statue of Cristobal Colom (Columbus) stands atop a 50 m high column of iron. Good views, best in morning, from platform. Nearby, in the harbour, is a replica of the Santa Maria caravel, his flagship on his first voyage to the Americas.

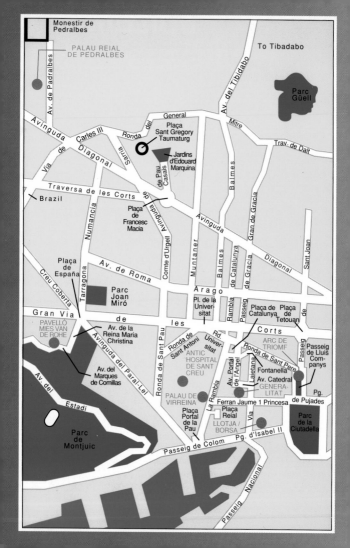

LLOTJA/BORSA Passeig d'Isabel II.
•Business hours. M. Barceloneta.
Barcelona's Stock Exchange. Original exchange hall (14thC) is preserved in the neo-classical building.

GENERALITAT Plaça Sant Jaume.
•General public only on 23 April. M. Jaume I.
Executive building of the Catalan government. Built to house the Generalitat, Western Europe's first parliament created in 1359. The main facade is Renaissance. Old facade (1416) with medallion of St George, is on Carrer Bisbe.

ANTIC HOSPITAL DE SANT CREU Hospital.
M Liceu.
Founded in the llthC, it is now a lovely group of buildings and courtyards which houses the Institut d'Estudis Catalans and the Biblioteca de Catalunya.

PALAU DE VIRREINA La Rambla 99.
Late l8thC palace. Houses the Cultural Information Centre, ticket office for cultural events, a collection of decorative arts and postal history exhibition. Also presents visiting art shows.

ARC DE TRIOMF Passeig de Lluis Companys.
M Arc de Triomf.
Designed by Joseph Vilaseca as the entrance to the 1888 Exhibition. An elaborate construction of unclad brick with ceramic decoration.

PALAU REIAL DE PEDRALBES Diagonal 686.
•1000-1300/1600-1900 Tues.-Fri., 1000-1330 Sat./Sun. M Palau Reial.
Barcelona's gift to Alfonso XIII. Pleasant gardens. Collection of paintings, tapestries, furniture, decorative arts. Carriage museum.

PAVELLÓ MIES VAN DE ROHE Avinguda Marquès de Comillas.
M Plaça de Espanya, then Bus 61.
German pavilion for the 1929 Exhibition named after its famous architect.

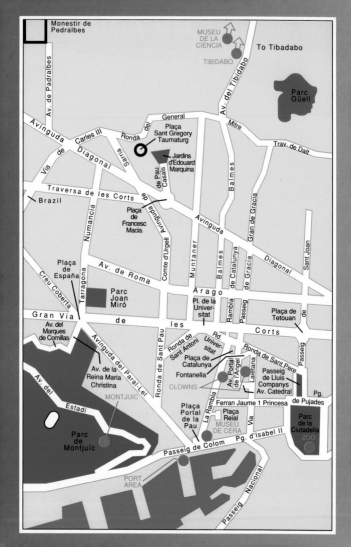

PORT AREA M Drassanes.
*Near the Plaça Portal de la Pau are quite a few attractions for children: Museu Maritim and Museu Cera (see **MUSEUMS**); Colom (Columbus) Monument (see **CHURCHES** etc); Carabela Santa Maria, the tiny ship in which Columbus braved unknown oceans; Torre de Jaume I, on Moll de Barcelona, for cable car rides (Telefèric) to Montjuïc or to Barceloneta.*

MONTJUIC
• 1200-2000 Sat., Sun., holidays. M Parallel, then Funicular, Telefèric.
The amusement park rides include ferris-wheel, roller-coaster, and the 'crazy rat' plus some sideshows for adults.

TIBIDABO
• 1100-2000 Sat., Sun., holidays. M Av del Tibidabo, then Tranvia Blau and Funicular.
Getting there on an old tram and the funicular is part of the fun. Although a bit dated, the park contains all the usual rides and thrills. There is also a museum of mechanical dolls.

ZOO Parc de la Ciutadella.
• 0930-1930. M Parc Ciutadella.
Floc de Neu, an albino gorilla, is star attraction among the captives. Other features: serpent house, aviary, infants' zoo, dolphin, killer-whale shows.

MUSEU DE LA CIÈNCIA Teodor Roviralta 55.
• 1000-2000 Tues.-Sun. M Tibidabo.
Science museum containing exhibits relating to Perception, Light, Waves, Mechanics, Computers and Meteorology. There is also a Planetarium.

MUSEU DE CERA Passatge de la Banco 7 (Rambla de Sta Monica).
• 1100-1330 and 1630-1930. M Drassanes.
Wax figures and tableaux. A historical and present day who's who.

CLOWNS M Plaça de Catalunya.
The Rambla Canaletes and Portal de l'Angel are two good places to find clowns and other street performers who delight young children.

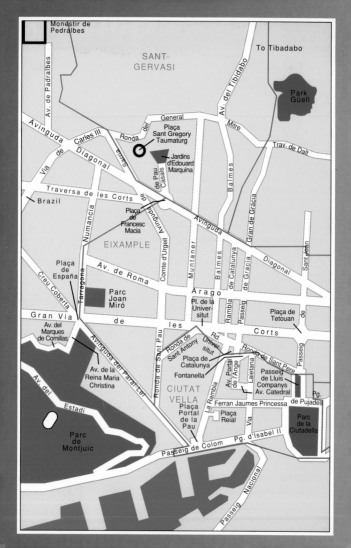

CITY DISTRICTS

City Districts are divided into barrios. *Short-term visitors are likely to find the following of most interest. See also* **PARKS**.

CIUTAT VELLA: The Old City. The harbourside *barrio* of **Barceloneta** is a grid pattern of tenement housing best know for its abundance of fish restaurants. Tourists throng La Rambla and the Barri Gòtic within the Ciutat Vella and Carrer Montcada in Sant Pere-Ribera. These parts are loaded with atmosphere and have many of the city's museums, budget hostels, traditional eateries and most-photographed corners. In other parts, decaying and sinister, poor people struggle to live decently while an exploitative, drug-based crime thrives. Strangers should be wary in the areas on the port side of Carrers de Hospital and Ferran, particularly after dark. Here too, all types of sex are for sale and the Barri Xines (**Laval** *barrio*) has been the red-light area for centuries..

EIXAMPLE: Large district of squared blocks and tree-lined avenues, intersected by the broad thoroughfares of Gran Vía de Les, Corts Catalanes and Avinguda Diagonal with the parallel, grand boulevards of Rambla Catalunya and Passeig de Gràcia at its centre. Much of it is very elegant and it's the heartland of Barcelona's progressive bourgeoisie. Many of the city's most prestigious addresses for apartments, hotels, shops and offices are here, especially in the **Dreta de L'Eixample** (Right Side). And this *barrio* also has many of the finest modernista buildings, best restaurants and top nightspots.

SANT GERVASI: Beyond Avinguda Diagonal, once separate villages of Gràcia, Sarria and Sant Gervasi were absorbed in the city's expansion. Parts retain a close community atmosphere. Socially they vary from the working-class quarters of Gràcia to the high-life homes of upper Sarria. You'll get a truer insight on contemporary Barcelona lifestyles around here than in touristy Ciutat Vella. The lower part of Sant Gervasi is very much 'in' with the well-connected, fashionable and young set, by day and night.

OPERATORS AND TERMINALS
Julia Tours, Ronda Universitat 5. M Universitat.
Pullmantur, Gran Via 635. M Plaça de Catalunya.
These offer similar tours and prices. Book with them or through hotels and travel agents. Itineraries can change. Men should wear a jacket and tie on night tours.

PANORAMIC
•Morning. Depart 0930 daily.
Visit Cathedral and Gothic Quarter, drive along waterfront and up to Montjuïc hill, visit Poble Espanyol.

GAUDÍ AND PICASSO
•Afternoon. Depart 1530 daily.
Drive along Passeig de Gràcia, seeing 'Manzana de la Discordia' and Casa Milà, then visit Güell Park. Stop to view Sagrada Família, before visiting Museu Picasso.

BULLFIGHT AND PANORAMIC
•Afternoon. Sundays and some weekdays during summer. Advance booking advised.
Depart one and a half hours before bullfight for a drive through the city.

FLAMENCO
•Night. Depart 2000 (to include dinner) or 2115 (show and drinks only). Not on Sundays or holidays.
Drive along main avenues, followed by a tablao flamenco.

SCALA BARCELONA
•Night. Depart 2000 (to include dinner) or 2115 (show and drinks only). Not on Sundays, Mondays and holidays.
Brief drive, followed by international show at city's biggest cabaret venue.

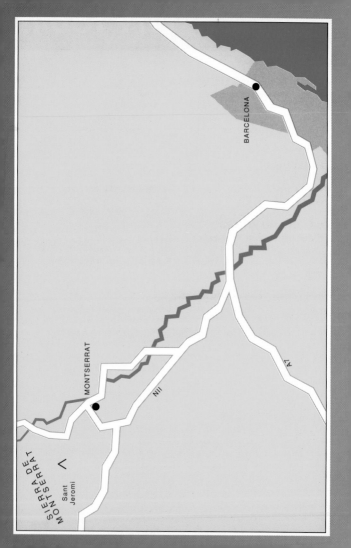

Montserrat

One day. Trains from station below Plaça Espanya.
By road 50 km west, Autopista A7, turn off at Exit 25.

The saw-toothed massif of Montserrrat, rising incongruously and
magically, above the surrounding countryside and River Llobregat, is
one of Spain's most impressive natural sights and is the spiritual heart
of Catalunya.

Its growth as a religious centre, so significant for Catalans and for
Catholics everywhere, began in 880 with the discovery in a cave of the
small statue, *La Moreneta*, the Black Virgin. Legend claims it was
carved by St Luke and first hidden by St Peter. Lost after the Moorish
invasion of the 8thC, it reappeared but refused to be taken from the
mountain. In 976, the Benedictines were charged with its protection
and they began building their monastery which over the centuries pros-
pered enormously, gaining an exceptional independence. A multitude
of miracles were attributed to this Virgin and many rulers and notables
made the pilgrimage to her. Nowadays she receives more tourists than
pilgrims although many Catalan baby girls are still christened
Montserrat and couples go to receive her blessing on their marriage.
During times of suppression of their Catalan identity, notably under
Franco, the Virgin, the monks and their institution offered Catalans
hope and succour.

Napoleon's troops had sacked the monastery in 1811, the Carlists had
suppressed it in 1835 and its end seemed final. But it revived and today
some 300 monks inhabit the new, barracks-like buildings.

In the Basilica (1560-92), La Moreneta has a chamber above the high
altar and the voices of the boys' choir, *La Escolania*, ring in their daily
performance of the Salve at 1300 hours (except July). There is a
Museum with minor paintings by old masters and another exhibition
area for l9thC Catalan artists.

If you want to escape the crowds the mountain has many options: it has
quiet paths, grand vistas and isolated hermitages - accessible on foot,
by funicular or by *telefèric*. It's an hour's walk to Sant Jeromi, the her-
mitage near the summit (1253 m), or reach it by a ride on the *telefèric*.
The monks run two good hostelries and there is also a campsite, youth
hostel, shops, market.

see **COACH TOURS**.

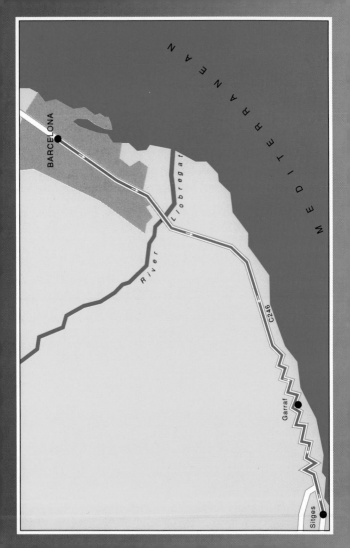

Sitges

Trains from Central-Sants; Bus from Estació del Nord; by car along C246 (road to airport).
• *Museums: 1000-1330 and 1630-1830 Tues.-Sun.*

Some 40 km south of the city, on the Costa Daurada, Sitges nestles between the Garraf mountains and a half-moon shoreline of good sand. It is the resort town where fashionable, monied Barcelonans take their seaside pleasures. They have done so for a long time. Thus, it has a well-established look and an air of elegance lacking in many resorts which have mushroomed in the tourist boom. Not that the building bonanza and international crowd have missed Sitges. There are many new hotels, apartment blocks and villas but they are mostly of a high standard and do not intrude on the delightful old town of whitewashed buildings which lies behind the long, palm-fringed promenade. Flowers abound. A rose coloured church stands on a small promontory above the fishing harbour. Nearby, marine facilities cater for yachts. Two well-kept beaches, serviced by balnearios, face the town. To the south are the rather unfortunately named Playas del Muerto (Beaches of the Dead) for nudists.

In 1892, Santiago Rusiol helped organise the town's first *Festes Modernistes* and his studio-museum, Cau Ferrat, became the mecca of modernisme. With the adjoining Museu Maricel, it can be visited to see a collection of works by Rusiol, other modernista artists, wrought iron pieces, ceramics, as well as two paintings by El Greco. The Museu Romántico (Casa Llopis) provides an insight into the life of a wealthy family in the l9thC.

You may be tempted by some boutiques or arts and crafts shops. There is a good choice of eating places, from basic beach bars, cool *terrazas* to very elegant restaurants. The nightlife is vibrant and anything goes. Bars and discos emulate the up-beat style of Barcelona's best. Many are exclusively gay.

In late May Sitges hosts the country's exhibition of carnations - Spain's national flower. Its Corpus Christi festivities are famous, the streets are laid with a bright carpet of flowers. In February, there's an antique car rally; in October, an international festival of avant-garde theatre; in November, the International Festival of Fantasy and Terror Films.

Tourist office: Plaça d'Eduard Maristany.

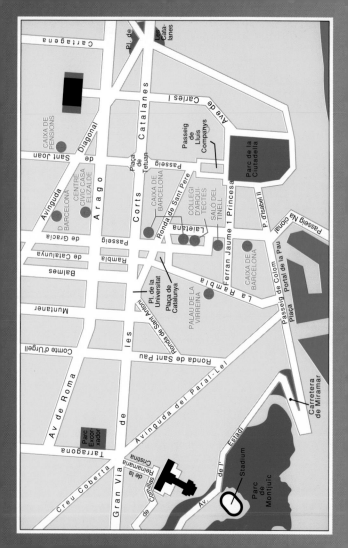

SALÓ DEL TINELL
Plaça del Rei (Barri Gòtic).
M Jaume I.
A large, Gothic hall which is an inspiring site for both exhibitions and performances.

COLLEGI D'ARQUITECTES
Plaça Nova.
M Jaume I, Plaça de Catalunya.
Exibitions relating to architecture - people and buildings.

PALAU DE LA VIRREINA
La Rambla 99.
M Liceu.
Cultural Information Centre and changing exhibitions.

D BARCELONA
Diagonal 367.
M Diagonal.
A store which not only sells the best in modern design objects but also has exhibitions.

CAIXA DE PENSIONS
Passeig Sant Joan 108.
Effective conversion of modernista building to spacious cultural centre. Also has exhibition centres at Montcada 14 and Via Laietana 56.

CAIXA DE BARCELONA
Arcs 5, Jaume I 2, Passeig de Gràcia 2.
Three locations of a bank which actively supports Barcelona's cultural life.

CENTRE CIVIC CASA ELIZALDE
València 302.
M Passeig de Gràcia.
Neighbourhood centre for a variety of cultural presentations.

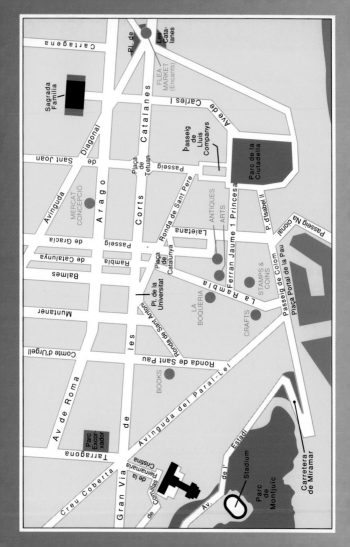

LA BOQUERIA La Rambla (Sant Josep). •Mon.-Sat. Ⓜ Liceu.
Within this ornamental ironwork building is one of the most fascinating food markets in Europe. There are impressive displays of an immense variety of high-quality produce and a bustling atmosphere created by the sellers and buyers .

MERCAT CONCEPCIÓ València/Girona.
•Mon.-Sat. Ⓜ Passeig de Gracia, Verdaguer.
A neighbourhood food market, smaller and less publicized than La Boqueria but as fascinating. Don't miss the flower stalls on Carrer València.

ANTIQUES Plaça Nova. •0900-2000 Thurs. Ⓜ. Liceu, Jaume I.
About 30 antique dealers show their wide variety of wares. Browse, bargain and buy. There's something, and a price, for everyone.

ART Plaça Sant Josep Oriol. •1100-2000 Sat., Sun. Ⓜ Liceu.
Colourful scene in a pretty square. Hopeful artists display their work, which is generally of a high standard.

BOOKS Mercat de Sant Antoni. •1000-1400 Sun. Ⓜ Poble Sec.
As a world capital for Spanish-language publishing, Barcelona should have a good second-hand books and magazines market - and this is it. Also comics, numismatic items.

STAMPS AND COINS Plaça Reial. •1000-1400 Sun. Ⓜ Liceu.
In this lovely square there's eager trading in stamps, old postcards and lottery tickets, coins and medals.

FLEAMARKET (ENCANTS) Plaça de les Glòries Catalanes.
•0800-1900 Wed., Fri., Sat. Ⓜ. Glories.
Second-hand goods, junk and, perhaps, a rare find.

CRAFTS Rambla Santa Mònica.
•1700-0100 Sat., Sun., holidays. Ⓜ Drassanes.
An assortment of present-day crafts. Remember, it's best to avoid this part of la Rambla after dark.

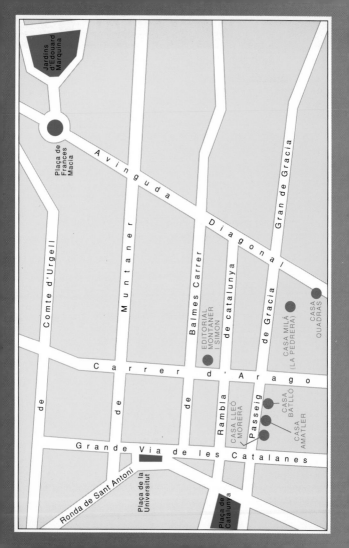

CASA LLEÓ MORERA Passeig de Gràcia 35.
Patronat Municipal de Turisme. •0900-1430 and 1530-1730 Mon.-Sat.
M Passeig de Gràcia.
Domenech i Montaner. 1905. Apartment house, now more interesting inside than outside. It's on 'la manzana de discordia', the block (or apple) of discord, where work by the three modernista masters is contrasted.

CASA AMATLER Passeig de Gràcia 41.
M Passeig de Gràcia.
Puig i Cadafalch. 1898. Remodelling of an apartment building. Flemish gable, facade decorated on theme of St George and the dragon.

CASA BATLLÓ Passeig de Gràcia 43.
M Passeig de Gràcia.
Gaudí. 1905-7. Renovated apartment building. Brilliant use of ceramics and the organic form. Typical of Gaudí.

EDITORIAL MONTANER I SIMON Aragó 255.
Fundació Tapies. M Passeig de Gràcia.
Domenech i Montaner. 1880. Mixes mudejar and contemporary elements. Uses iron and unclad masonry. After renovation will reopen as the Fundació Tapies - a modern art exhibition and study centre.

CASA MILÁ (LA PEDRERA) Passeig de Gràcia 92.
Visits under auspices of Fundació Caixa de Catalunya/UNESCO:
•1000,1100,1200,1600,1700 Mon.-Fri.; 1000,1100,1200 Sat.;
1100,1200 1st and 3rd Sun. of month. M Diagonal.
Gaudí. 1905-10. Unclad stone hung on iron frame and sculpted in mobile shapes and flowing lines. Iron balconies like seaweed. A roofline of pale tiles and twisted chimneys.

CASA QUADRAS Diagonal 373.
See **Museu de la Música**. M Diagonal.
Puig i Cadafalch. 1904. Compact, elegant house. Some design elements similar to those of his large medieval-looking apartment block, Casa Terrades, 1903-1905, almost opposite on the Diagonal.

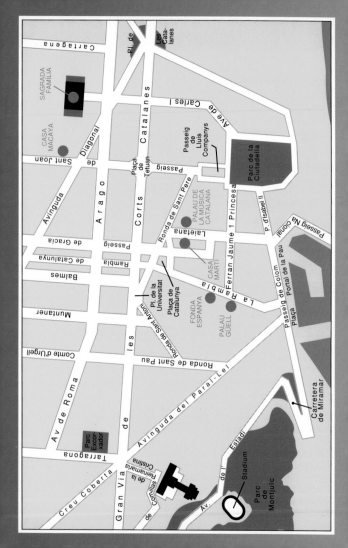

CASA MACAYA Passeig de Sant Joan 108.
•Hours vary Centre Cultural de la Caixa de Pensions.
Ⓜ Verdaguer.
Puig i Cadafalch. 1901. Residence, successfully converted to cultural centre. Notable sculptured decoration, courtyard and covered stairway.

SAGRADA FAMÍLIA Plaça de la Sagrada Família.
•0900-1900. Elevator in Façana de la Pasió 1000-1345, 1500-1845.
Ⓜ Sagrada Família.
Gaudí. 1883-1926. Unfinished project of a genius consumed by his religiosity. Great architectural legacy or the misconceived indulgence of a madman? Should work stop or continue? It will not leave you unmoved. Small museum.

PALAU GÜELL Nou de Rambla 3. Ciutat Vella.
Museu del Teatre. •1100-1400, 1700-2000 Mon.-Sat. Ⓜ Liceu.
Gaudí. 1886-88. Town house of his patron with large, central salon, impressive staircase and lots of intriguing details.

FONDA ESPANYA Sant Pau 9. Ciutat Vella.
Hotel foyer, generally open. Dining room, meal times. Ⓜ Liceu.
Domenech i Montaner. 1902-03. Hotel's ground-floor decoration by Domenech, Eusebi Arnau (sculptor) and Ramón Casas (painter).

CASA MARTÍ Montsio 3.Ciutat Vella.
See **RESTAURANTS**, Els Quatre Gats. Ⓜ Plaça de Catalunya.
Puig i Cadafalch. 1895-96. Apartment block. His early style, combining inspiration from Catalan and other Gothic art.

PALAU DE LA MÚSICA CATALANA Sant Peres mes Alt.
Ciutat Vella.
During performances. Ⓜ Urquinaona.
Domenech i Montaner. 1905-08. Inside and outside, it's the epitome of modernista architecture's richly decorative expression. Stained glass, ceramics, sculpture and painting, all combined to convey the integration of the arts.

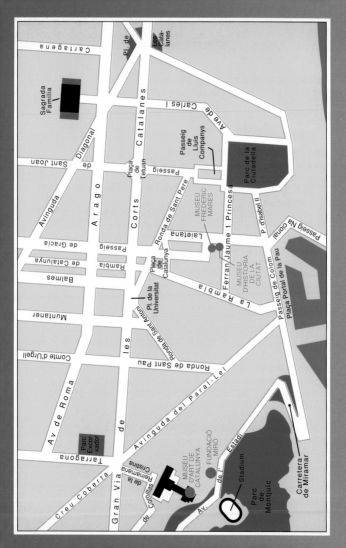

MUSEU D'ART DE CATALUNYA
Palau Nacional (Montjuïc).
•0900-1400 Tues.-Sun.
Ⓜ Plaça d'Espanya, then Bus 61 from Avda. Maria Cristina.
Wonderfully rich collections of Catalan Romanesque and Gothic art are perfectly displayed within the huge Palau Nacional building. Romanesque frescoes and altar pieces saved from decaying churches. Painted panels and carved figures showing the separateness of Catalan Gothic. There's an adjoining Ceramics Museum.

FUNDACIÓ MIRÓ
Plaça Neptú (Montjuïc).
•1100-2000 Tues.-Sat., 1100-1430 Sun. and hols.
Ⓜ Plaça de'Espanya, then Bus 61 from Avda. Maria Cristina.
Housed in architect Josep Luis Sert's successful building there are permanent displays of Joan Miró's work and also a collection donated by contemporary artists from around the world. In addition there are temporary exhibitions, concerts and other cultural events plus a library, a bookshop, and a cafeteria.

MUSEU D'HISTORIA DE LA CIUTAT
Plaça del Rei (Barri Gòtic).
•0900-2030 Tues.-Sat., 0900-1330 Sun. and hols.
Ⓜ Jaume I.
In a 16thC Gothic palace above archaeological excavations. Exhibits chronicle the city's history.

MUSEU FREDERIC MARES
Plaça de Sant Iu (Barri Gòtic).
•0900-1400, 1600-1900 Tues.-Sat., 0900-1400 Sun. and hols.
Ⓜ Jaume I.
The collection of this magpie sculptor is assembled in what was once the palace of the Counts of Barcelona. The collection contains stone sculpture from the 10th to 16thC. Romanesque and Gothic painting and carvings, and an amazing variety of objects, everyday and obscure, gathered over 50 years of travelling.

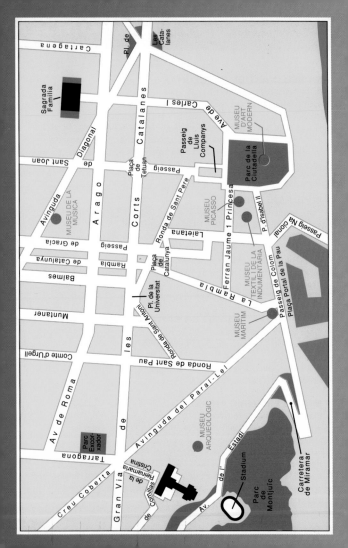

MUSEU PICASSO
Montcada 15-17.
•1600-2030 Mon., 0900-1400 and 1600-2030 Tues.-Sat., 0900-1400 Sun. and hols. M Jaume I.
Displayed in two converted palaces, the collection is strongest on his juve-nilia, blue, pink, cubist and neo-classical periods. Also his studies of Velázquez's Las Meninas.

MUSEU D'ART MODERN
Parc de la Ciutadella.
•1500-1930 Mon., 0900-1930 Tues.-Sat., 0900-1400 Sun. and hols.
Catalan painters and sculptors. Early l9th century to modern times.

MUSEU MARÌTIM
Plaça Portal de la Pau.
•1000-1400 and 1600-1900 Tues.-Sat., 1000-1400 Sun. and hols.
M Drassanes.
Medieval dockyards with a varied display of things nautical. Replica of the grand galley which led Spain's fleet in the battle of Lepanto, 1571.

MUSEU DE LA MÚSICA
Diagonal 373.
•0900-1400 Tues.-Sun. M Diagonal.
Musical instruments in an elegant modernista mansion by Puig i Cadafalch.

MUSEU ARQUEOLÒGIC
Passeig Sta Madrona/Leida (Montjuic).
•0930-1300 and 1600-1900 Tues.-Sat., 0930-1400 Sun. and hols. M Plaça d'Espanya, then Bus 61 from Avda Maria Cristina.
Most notable are the megalithic collections from Majorca, Punic finds from Ibiza and sculpture from the Greek settlement of Empuries (Costa Brava).

MUSEU TEXTIL I DE LA INDUMENTÀRIA
Montcada 12.
•0900-1400 and 1630-1900 Tues.-Sat. M Jaume I.
Lovely 15thC palaces house displays of textiles, lace and curtains.

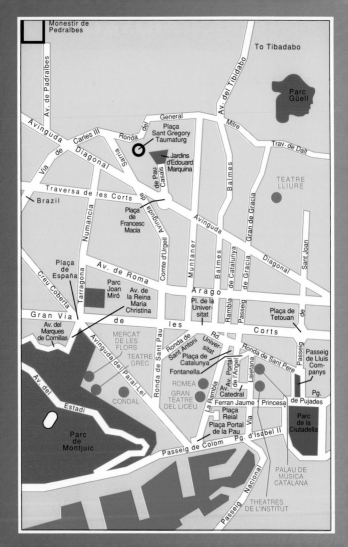

CONDAL Parallel 91-93.
M Paral.lel.
Another venue for innovative theatre.

THEATRES DE L'INSTITUT Sant Peres mes Baix 7.
M Urquinaona.
Two spaces presenting drama and dance. Mostly contemporary works.

TEATRE GREC Passeig Santa Madrona (Montjuïc).
Replica of a Greek theatre built for 1929 Exhibition. Principal venue for the well-supported Greek festival of music and dance each July.

TEATRE LLIURE Montseny 47 (Gràcia).
M Fontana.
A company with a reputation for presenting some of the most exciting theatre in the Spanish language. Restaurant.

MERCAT DE LES FLORS Leida 59 (Montjuïc).
Built as an exhibition hall for the 1929 Exhibition. Under the auspices of the Ayuntament de Barcelona, this is now a high-tech venue for a variety of theatrical presentations. Tickets from Palau de Virreina, La Rambla.

ROMEA Hospital 5. M Liceu.
Home of the Centre Dramàtic de la Generalitat. The Catalan government sponsors much new and exciting theatre here.

PALAU DE MÚSICA CATALANA Sant Pere mes Alt.
M Urquinaona.
Perhaps the world's most fascinating concert hall. Centre of the city's musical life and the International Music Festival each October.
See **MODERNISME 2.**

GRAN TEATRE DEL LICEU La Rambla 61.
•Visits: 1130 and 1215 Mon., Wed., Fri. Closed Jul.-Sep. M Liceu.
Built mid-l9thC. Elegant venue presenting the best of Spanish and international opera (Nov.-Mar.) and ballet (Apr.-Jun.).

BARRI GÒTIC

Sightseeing gem of well-preserved Gothic buildings.
See WALKS.

BULEVARD ROSA

Shoppers' paradise in a mall of many, varied shops.
See SHOPPING, **Eixample.**

MUSEU D'ART DE CATALUNYA

Outstanding collections of Romanesque and Gothic art.
See MUSEUMS.

FUNDACIÓ MIRÓ

Outstanding, modern building containing works by Miró and others. Good, changing cultural events. See MUSEUMS.

LA RAMBLA

Stroll on one of the world's most animated streets.
See WALKS.

SAGRADA FAMÍLIA

What will be your opinion of Gaudí's unfinished cathedral?
See MODERNISME 2.

PARC GÜELL

Views across the city from another Gaudí creation.
See PARKS.

PALAU DE LA MÚSICA

Join an audience in the world's most flamboyant concert hall.
See MUSIC.

ZELESTE

The popular, multi-event venue of Barcelona's exuberant contemporary culture and entertainment scene.
See NIGHTLIFE 2.

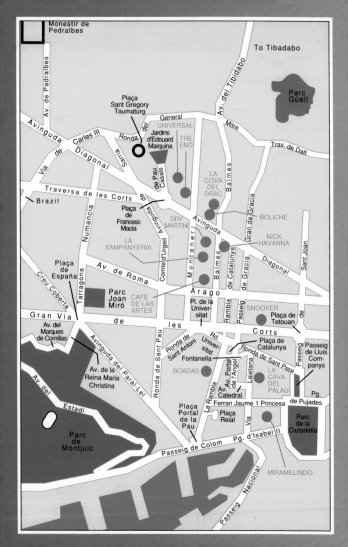

Bars

NICK HAVANNA Roselló 208.
Chic, youthful effervescence. Great lighting and sounds, attentive service.

SNOOKER Roger de Lluria 42.
Has Steve Davis been here? Cocktail mixers who know their stuff.

BOLICHE Diagonal 510.
Big, 50s decor and a bowling alley as a distraction.

LA COVA DEL DRAC Tuset 30.
Relaxed atmosphere and the best venue for live jazz.

CAFÈ DE LAS ARTES València 234.
Music, video and a mixed, fashionable crowd.

THE END Santaló 34.
Very 'in' on the Barcelona night scene. Good sounds and videos.

UNIVERSAL Maria Cubi 184.
Big place. Best atmosphere on the first floor. Also has concerts and shows.

MIRAMELINDO Passeig del Born 15.
Tropical atmosphere in the best of a number of bars along this street.

BOADAS Tallers l.
Small and unpretentious, with barmen who make superb cocktails.

DRY MARTINI Corsega/d'Aribau.
Trendsetter of its type, this cocktail lounge will set the tone for the night.

LA CAVA DEL PALAU Verdaguer i Callís 10.
Cavas, cocktails and light meals near to the Palau de la Música.

LA XAMPANYERIA Provença 236.
Good starting point for a night out in the Eixample. Elegant, refined service.

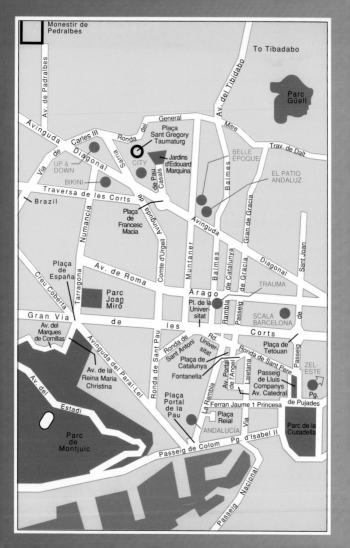

UP AND DOWN
Numància 179.
Jet-set crowd. Upstairs (men need ties), grand disco, young set downstairs.

ZELESTE
Almogavers 122.
Disco, restaurant, terrace, video shows. Features the best of modern bands and jazz groups from Spain and abroad. Highly recommended.

CITY
Beethoven 15.
What would Beethoven say? Great music, lights, lively, new-wave people.

BIKINI
Diagonal 571.
Lots of young, single people. Programme of varied live music.

TRAUMA
Consell de Cent 288.
An old favourite. A crowd which is less self-consciously fashionable.

EL PATIO ANDALUZ
Aribau 242.
Aficionados enjoy the colour and movement of sevillanas and flamenco.

ANDALUCÍA
La Rambla 27.
More tourists here. Good shows of flamenco dancing.

SCALA BARCELONA
Three restaurants.
Big place with an international cabaret spectacular.

BELLE EPOQUE
Muntaner 246.
More intimate and local flavour. Reputation for most imaginative cabarets.

MONTJUÏC

M Plaça Espanya, Bus 61 and 201. M Paral.lel, Bus 201, Funicular.
From Barceloneta by Telefèric.
*This gently rising mound of greenery and lovely gardens is packed with
places of interest -- culture, sports and entertainment -- as well as quiet,
shady places for relaxation. Most of the buildings were put up for the 1929
Exhibition. The Olympic Stadium will be the focus of 1992's Games.*

PARC DE LA CIUTADELLA

M Arc de Triomf.
*The Ciutadella was a huge fort built by the first Bourbon king. Destroyed
and turned into a park in the 1870s, it was the staging ground for the 1888
Exhibition. A monumental cascade on which Gaudí worked rises above a
small boating pond. Remaining Bourbon buildings house the Catalan
Parliament and Museum of Modern Art. The Zoo takes up part of the park
(see* **CHILDREN***).*

JARDÍNS D'EDUARD MARQUINA Avinguda de Pau Casals.

Bus 66 from Plaça Catalunya.
Formal gardens with small pond in the heart of this posh shopping area.

PARC GÜELL Olot s/n.

M Lesseps, then Bus 24 from Plaça Catalunya.
*In the communal area of what was intended to be a garden suburb, Gaudí
let his imagination run riot. Working with Jujol, between 1900 and 1914,
he completed two gatehouses, a grand stairway and a vast terrace with its
famous, snaking bench of glittering mosaics. Hewn in stone on site, are
paths, viaducts, porticos, columns.*

TIBIDABO

F Tibidabo, then Tranvia Blau (tram), then Funicular. Bus 17 from Plaça
Catalunya, then Tranvia Blau etc.
*High point (530 m) of the Collserola range. On good days there are wide
views of the city, and towards Montserrat and the Pyrenees, sometimes even
to Mallorca. Amusement park and restaurants. Also forested area in which
to escape the crowds.*

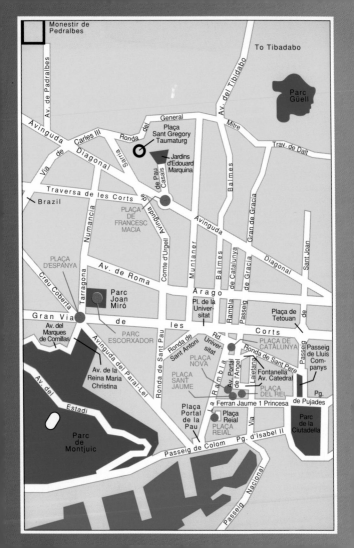

PLAÇA DE CATALUNYA M Catalunya.
*Central, busy hub between the oldest and newer parts. Big, open square sur-
rounded by many banks. A clock of flowers.*

PLAÇA NOVA Barri Gòtic.
*Architectural mix of Roman towers, baroque episcopal palace and the
College of Architects with decoration by Picasso and Miró.*

PLAÇA DEL REI Barri Gòtic.
*Courtyard of the former royal palace and the city's most evocative and
handsome ensemble of Gothic architecture. Left from the entrance is the
Palau de Lloctinent and, to the right, the Casa Clariana/Padellós .*

PLAÇA DE SANT JAUME Barri Gòtic.
*Facing each other across this partly pedestrianized square are the grand
civic buildings of the Generalitat and Ayuntament, headquarters of the
regional and city governments respectively. Most interesting facade of the
Generalitat is on Carrer Bisbe (15thC), that of the Ayuntament on Carrer de
la Ciutat (14thC).*

PLAÇA REIAL off Rambla de Capuchín. M Liceu.
Rectangle of neo-classical arcaded buildings, palm trees, lamps by Gaudi.

PLAÇA D'ESPANYA M Espanya.
*Busy intersection of Gran Via de les Corts Catalanes and Avinguda del
Paral.lel. Entry point for the Fira de Barcelona (Trade Fairs and Congresses)
and Montjuic hill. Also here, the city's older bullring, Les Arenes.*

PARC ESCORXADOR M Espanya.
*Dominated by Miro's huge, bovine monolith, this is an example of the city's
many 'urbanism' projects - urban enhancement through landscaping, sculpture and architecture.*

PLAÇA DE FRANCESC MACIA
Bus 66.
Elegant circle on Avinguda Diagonal in smart, uptown district.

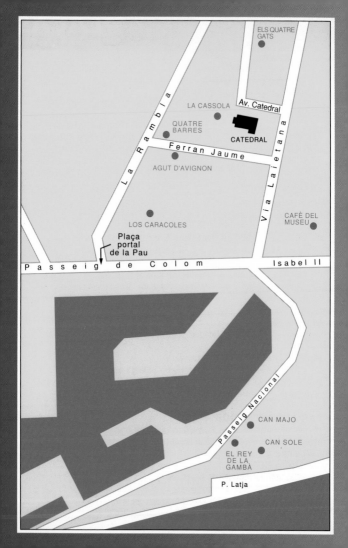

Ciutat Vella

EL REY DE LA GAMBA Passeig Nacional 46-48.
• Closed Mon. • Budget.
A good choice among the string of places along the Passeig Nacional.

CAN MAJO Almirall Aixada 23.
• Closed Mon. and Aug. • Moderate.
Smartest place in the area. Superb rice-based specialities and seafood.

CAN SOLE San Carlos 4.
• Closed Sat. night and Sun. First two weeks Feb. and Sept. • Budget.
Best make a reservation for lunch at this old, family-run favourite. As in most Barceloneta restaurants, the choice of fresh seafood is tantalising.

CAFÈ DEL MUSEU Montcada 15 (Museu Picasso).
• Closed evenings and Mon. • Budget.
Impeccable cooking, imaginative dishes, good service.

ELS QUATRE GATS Montsió 3.
• Closed Sun. • Moderate.
In the modernista building where Picasso met with his artist friends.

QUATRE BARRES Quintana 6.
• Budget. Reservations.
Impeccable restaurant giving excellent value.

AGUT D'AVIGNON D'Avinyó/La Trinitat.
• Moderate.
Evocative, old place with innovative, Catalan cooking and good cellar.

LOS CARACOLES Escudellers 14.
• Budget.
Grills and basic cooking in a busy tavern which attracts a lot of tourists.

LA CASSOLA Sant Sever 3.
One of the many basic, weekday eateries within the Barri Gòtic catering to locals and tourists with set menus under l,000 pesetas.

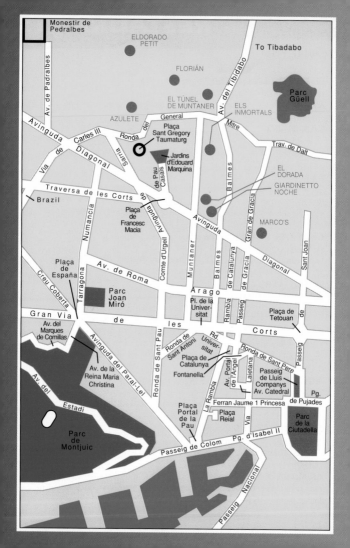

Diagonal

EL DORADA Travessera de Gràcia 44.
•Closed Sun. •Expensive.
Nautical decor and Andalucian flavour. Simply prepared, top quality fish and seafood specialities. Also, superb rice dishes.

ELDORADO PETIT Dolors Monserda 51.
•Closed Sun. •Expensive.
One of Spain's top restaurants. Perfectly prepared foods from a varied menu of international cuisines.

FLORIÁN Bertrand i Serra 20.
•Closed Sun. •Expensive.
Adventurous, modern Catalan cooking at its best.

AZULETE Via Augusta 281.
•Closed Sat. lunch and Sun. •Moderate.
Town house with terrace and conservatory dining area. Eclectic, nouvellé cuisine menu with regional favourites.

EL TÚNEL DE MUNTANER San Marió 22.
•Closed Sat. lunch and Sun. •Moderate.
Spacious, refined place to enjoy the best products of the market prepared with precision. A neighbourhood favourite.

GIARDINETTO NOCHE Granada del Penedès 22.
•1930-0230. Closed Sun. •Moderate.
Sophisticated decor, service and cooking. Gentle live music.

MARCO'S Bonavista 10.
•Closed Sun. •Budget.
Great value lunch menu. Always packed. Young chef with a delicate touch.

ELS INMORTALS Marco Aurelio 27.
•Closed Sun. •Budget.
Regional variation of Italian dishes. Bright, welcoming and very popular in the neighbourhood.

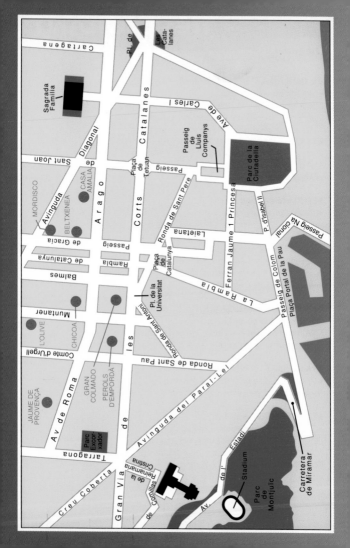

Eixample

BELTXENEA Mallorca 275.
•Closed Sat. lunch and Sun. •Expensive.
Best of Basque cuisine in an elegant, townhouse setting.

JAUME DE PROVENÇA Provença 88.
•Closed Sun. night, Mon. •Expensive.
Nothing outstanding about the decor or service but high ratings for its classic cooking with inspired deviations.

GRAN COLMADO Consell de Cent 318.
•Closed Sun. and hols. •Moderate.
Top restaurant where seeing and being seen is as important as the food.

CHICOA Aribau 73.
•Sun. and hols. •Moderate.
Farmhouse decoration. Bacalao dishes are the speciality. Good choice of other fish, meat and vegetables.

CASA AMALIA Pasatge Mercat Concepció 4.
•Closed Sun. night and Mon. •Budget.
Everything is fresh from the market opposite. Hearty, friendly atmosphere and honest cooking. Great value.

MORDISCO Rosselló 265.
•Closed Sun. •Budget.
Bright and buzzing from 0830 to 0200. Youngish, fashionable crowd enjoy the capricious menu and its surprises.

PEROLS D'EMPORDÀ Villarroel 88.
•Sun. night and Mon. •Moderate.
Small and traditional. Specialises in cuisine of the Ampurdan area (Gerona province) which is known for its rich gastronomy.

L'OLIVE Muntaner 171.
•Moderate.
Very popular brasserie. Efficient service of seasonal produce.

EIXAMPLE

M Plaça Catalunya, Passeig de Gràcia, Diagonal.

If your time for shopping is very limited, go straight to number 55 Passeig de Gràcia where the Bulevard Rosa has 70 small shops offering the latest fashions, accessories, designer items, knick-knacks and the rest. Upstairs, the Centro de Anticuarios has a similar number of antiques specialists. Here too is Centre Permanent d'Artesania de la Generalitat de Catalunya with the best of the region's craft items.Galeria Halley at Passeig de Gràcia 62 and La Avenida at Rambla Catalunya 121 are two more high-class shopping precincts. These broad avenues are the central arteries of this shopping district which has most of the top shops for clothes, jewellery, leather, art, modern design, decorative objects and housewares. Concentrate on the area between Carrers Balmes and Roger Lluria and crossed by Carrers Aragó, València, Mallorca, Provença and Rosseló.

SANT GERVASI

Bus 66 from Plaça Catalunya.

New mecca of the fashion trendsetters situated between Carrer Muntaner, Avinguda Diagonal, Carrer Ganduxer and Via Augusta. Prestigious shops, many small boutiques. Some super food shops too. Also, three shopping precincts: Diagonal Centre, Diagonal 584, first of its type in the city; Via Wagner, Bori i Fontesta 17; Turo Centre, Tenor Vinyas 14. And don't miss these streets: Avingusa Pau Casals, Carrers Mestre Nicolau, Ferran Agullo, Josep Bertrand, Santa Fe de Nou Mexic, Laforja, Calaf.

CIUTAT VELLA

M Plaça Catalunya, Liceu, Jaume I.

The most rewarding part is in the Ciutat Vella between Plaça de Catalunya, La Rambla, Carrer Ferrán, and Via Laietana. Main attraction is the variety of small shops selling modern, traditional and antique things, some useful, others quaint and quirky. Spend delightful hours wandering the maze of streets, popping into the shops which take your fancy. La Canuda, Santa Ana, Comtal, Portal de L'Angel are the smarter pedestrianized streets. Portaferrissa has a few good boutiques. At the corner of Santa Ana and Portal de L'Angel there's a Galerías Preciados store. Nearby, facing Plaça de Catalunya, is the big branch of the more up-market El Corte Inglés.

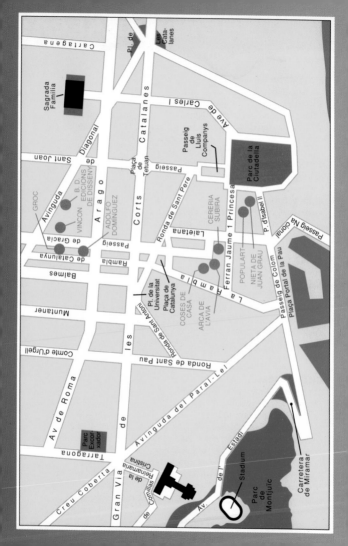

GROC
Rambla de Catalunya 100.
Two leading designers: Tony Miró (clothes) and Chelo Sastre (accessories) .

ADOLFO DOMÍNGUEZ
Passeig de Gràcia 89 and València 245.
Creations for women and men from the top international star of Spain's modern fashion flowering.

POPULART
Montcada 22.
Modern craft items in paper, papiermache, wood and ceramics.Ideal as gifts.

NIETA DE JUAN GRAU
Vidrieria 6.
A glass factory for 230 years. Shops sell a fascinating range of items.

CERERIA SUBIRA
Baixada Llibreteria 7.
They've been making candles here since 1761. All shapes, sizes,colours.

ARCA DE L'AVIA
Banys Nous 20.
Finest, very old and new lacework in a wide price range.

COSES DE CASA
del Pinó 5.
Cotton and linen household goods, finely made by hand.

B. D. EDICIONS DE DISSENY
Mallorca 291.
Furniture, lighting and housewares by leading designers.

VINCON
Passeig de Gràcia.
State of the art stuff for homemakers: well-priced housewares, furniture etc.

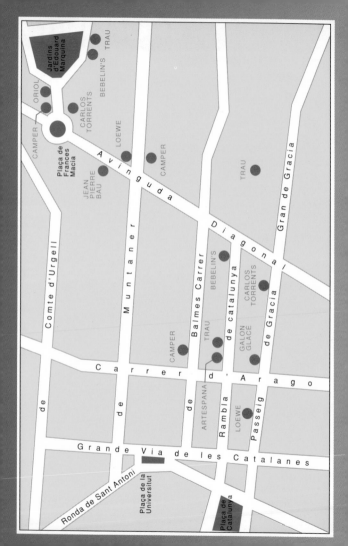

ARTESPANA
Rambla Catalunya 75.
Branch of the state-sponsored chain, sells a range of Spanish arts and crafts.

ORIOL
Bori i Fontesta 11.
Highly original jewellery by the talented Ramon Oriol.

BEBELIN'S
Galerias La Avenida (Rambla Catalunya 121), Tenor Vi.
High fashion for tiny tots and children up to 14 years.

CAMPER
València 246, Muntaner 248, Avinguda Pau Casals 5.
Wide selection of fashionable shoes.

GALON GLACÉ
Bulevard Rosa (Passeig de Gràcia 55).
Rated as a top shop for fashion accessories, notably those of Maria Araujo.

TRAU
València 260, Via Augusta 16, Ferran Agulló 6.
Women's fashions. Designs of Purificación García feature among prestigious labels. Trau Bàsic in Via Augusta is more for the younger set.

CARLOS TORRENTS
Paseo de Gràcia 95, Avinguda Pau Casals 6.
Well-designed shops stocking expensive 'in' clothes for men.

JEAN PIERRE BAU
Diagonal 469.
Fashions by designers like Agatha Ruiz de la Prada and Roser Marce.

LOEWE
Passeig de Gràcia 35, Diagonal 574.
Established internationally, sedate and elegant fashions; highest quality.

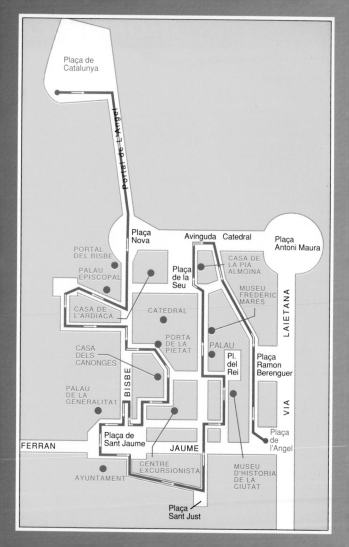

Barri Gòtic

M Plaça de Catalunya. **l.45 hr**
Walk down the shopping avenue of Portal de l'Angel to Pl Nova. Two
round towers of the Roman city's wall and the 13thC Palau Episcopal
flank the Portal del Bisbe. Behind is the 15thC Casa de l'Ardiaca
(Archdeacon), its handsome courtyard entered from c/Santa Llucia.
Right from c/Bisbe, where buskers entertain, leads to the enchanting Pl
Sant Felip Neri. Pass through and left into c/ Sant Sever. A right then a
left brings you to the Cathedral's Porta de la Pietat, opening to the
Cloister. 30 min
Opposite is the restored Casa dels Canonges (Canons). Follow it around
to the right. At c/Paradis 10, the Centre Excursionista has some remaining columns of a Roman temple. At Pl de Sant Jaume turn right into
c/Bisbe to see the old facade of the Generalitat on the left and the
reproduction Gothic passageway above the alley. Return to the *plaça*,
always an active place and stroll into the Ayuntament's courtyard. 15
min.
Leave by c/ de la Ciutat opposite. Original Gothic facade of the
Ayuntament is just on the right, go left into c/ d'Hercules to Pl Sant Just
dominated by the old parish church of royalty. Left again into c/
Dagueria, ahead of c/ Llibreteria, then turn right then left. The Museu
d'Historia de la Ciutat is well worth a visit. It forms one side of the Pl
del Rei, a very beautiful assembly of Gothic buildings and one of the
city's greatest treasures. 30 min
Leaving, turn right in c/ dels Comtes. A doorway leads to the garden of
the old royal palace and the Museu Frederic Mares with its varied,
interesting collections. Moving on, the Pl de la Seu and the main
entrance to the cathedral are on the left. On the right, is the Casa de la
Pia Almoina, built in the 15thC as a residence for the clergy and to
house a charity. It absorbed part of the Roman walls. Follow the preserved walls along c/ Tapineria to Pl de Ramon Berenguer where there's
an equestrian statue by Jose Llimona of the Catalan hero, Ramon
Berenguer III.
Finish at Pl de l'Angel and M Jaume I. 30 min

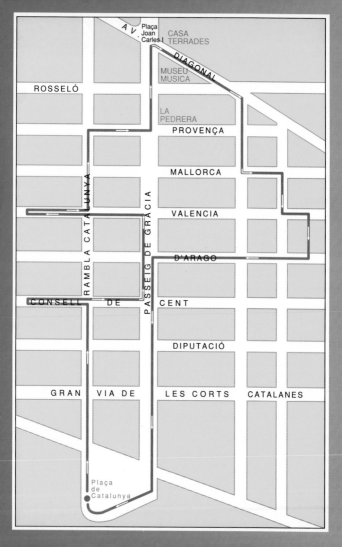

Eixample

M Plaça de Catalunya. **2.30 hr.**

Leave the plaça on the south west into broad Rambla Catalunya. Left at c/ Consell de Cent where there's a block of many art galleries. Retrace your steps, crossing Rambla Catalunya to reach Casa Lleo Morera on the corner of Passeig de Gracia (35). A *modernista* building in which the Municipal Tourist Office is located. 20 min.

Go left up Passeig de Gracia to see the other two buildings of the *manzana de la discordia* (block of discord), Puig's Casa Amatler (41) and Gaudi's Casa Batllo (43). On the next block, the shopping arcades of Bulevard Rosa and the Centro de Anticuarios (55) will no doubt tempt you in, at least for a stroll and some window-shopping. Note the wrought iron lamps and benches along the Passeig. 30 min.

Turn left into c/ Valencia which, up to c/ Balmes, has a number of good fashion shops. Return to Rambla Catalunya and turn left again. Here there are terrazas to take a rest and some sustenance and see more good shops like Groc (100). Go right at c/ Provenca to come to Gaudi's *La Pedrera* (The Quarry), opposite on Passeig de Gracia (92), where you'll probably want to linger. 40 min.

Continue up Passeig de Gracia to Pl Joan Carles I. Head right into Diagonal to the Museu Musica in Puig's Casa Quadras. Across the road is his pointed Casa Terrades. (Throughout this walk, keep your eyes open for many, lesser-known modernista buildings and features). Turn right into c/ Roger de Lluria to c/ Palau Montaner, base of the central government's delegation. Right for a few steps to another Domenech building (Mallorca 291), now B. D. Edicions's showrooms of modern design. 30 min.

Right once more into c/ del Bruc, left into c/ Valencia. Opposite is the *modernista* building of the Municipal School of Music. Bright flower stalls are in front of the Mercat Concepcio. Walk through the bustling market where foodstuffs are so attractively displayed. Exit on c/ d'Arago, take a right turn to Passeig de Gracia, then turn left. Have another look at the *manzana de la discordia* across the avenue. Walk down the side if you wish to be tempted by more shops, or down the middle if all you want to do is take a gentle *paseo* and indulge in some people-watching.

Finish at Plaça de Catalunya. 30 min

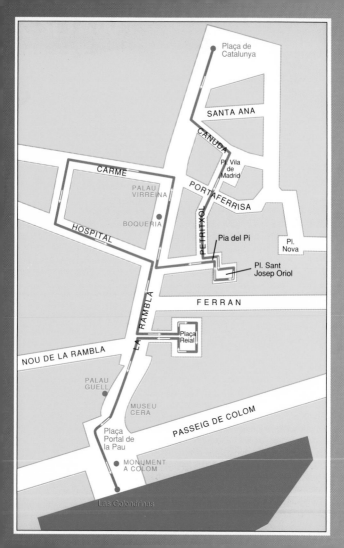

La Rambla

La Rambla comprises five linked streets with a wide central walkway lined with plane trees where a cosmopolitan crowd parades. This itinerary makes some detours from La Rambla. **2hrs**

M Plaça de Catalunya. On the right as you exit from the metro, there's the little Font de Canaletes. Drink from it and, so the legend goes, you're sure to return to Barcelona. Around here, street performers stake their pitch. To your left, c/ Santa Ana has a good choice of places to take a quick meal. Take c/ Canuda, past the Ateneo and turn right through quiet Pl Vila de Madrid to c/ Portaferrisa where there is some interesting shopping. There are more shops along c/ Petritxol, which leads to Pia del Pi and Pl Sant Josep Oriol where artists and students gather in the shadow of the Gothic church. c/ Cardenal Casasas leads back to La Rambla. The mosaic on the central pavement is by Miró. Casa Quadros, a *modernista* building by Vilaseca (now a bank), is on the right. 45 min

Notice the ornate *modernista* shopfront of the Antiga Casa Figueras grocery shop on the left. Then you come to La Boqueria, the most fascinating food market imaginable. Next is the Palau Virreina, notable building and cultural centre. At the old Jesuit church of Belen, go left into c/ Carme to reach the fine Gothic buildings of the Hospital de la Sant Creu, founded in the llthC and now mostly used for cultural and educational purposes. Walk through quiet courtyards and gardens to exit on c/ de Hospital. Turn left to La Rambla. 45 min

Walk right, past the plain exterior of the Teatre Liceu opera house. From here on, strollers should be more wary of pickpockets and bag snatchers. On the left a small passage opens into the Pl Reial, a pretty place but sometimes a bit menacing. Opposite, on c/ Nou de la Rambla, the Palau Guell by Gaudí is not to be missed. Carry on down La Rambla. This part was once the city's theatreland. The *modernista* La Pitarra monument commemorates the founder of modern Catalan drama. An alley leads to the Museu Cera (Wax Museum). The Palau March is an exhibition centre. La Rambla ends in the Pl Portal de la Pau (Gate of Peace) from which the monument to Columbus rises. On the right are the medieval shipyards (Museu Maritim). In the port there is a replica of Columbus's flagship and *Las Golondrinas* which make short cruises across the harbour. M Drassanes. 30 min

Accommodation: A great many new places of accommodation are being built, and existing ones upgraded, in preparation for the 1992 Olympics. The following are the main types of accommodation: Hoteles -H- are rated from one to five stars with Gran Lujo the very top rating. A *Hotel Apartamento* -HA- offers full hotel services with accommodation in apartments. A *Hotel Residencia* -HR- does not have a full restaurant. *Hostales* -HS- are much like hotels, usually with more modest facilities, and are rated one to three stars. But a good *hostal* can sometimes beat a similarly rated hotel. Tourist Apartments -AT- are rated from one to four keys, have self-catering facilities and usually require a minimum stay of one week. Guest Houses (*Casa de Huespedes*) and Inns (*Fondas*) offer the most basic accommodation.

The city has two youth hostels. Camping and Caravan sites (rated Categories 1 to 3) are plentiful along the coast, nearest to the city are those at El Prat and Esplugas de Llobregat (7 km). The Tourist Offices at the Airport and Gran Via can assist with finding accommodation. Spain's National Tourist Offices in your country will give information (but not make reservations). They can provide names of companies in your country which deal with reservations in Spain.

The Federació Catalana de Campings is at Via Laietana 59.

Airport: El Prat de Llobregat International Airport (*aeropuerto*) is 14 km south of the city. Porters are helpful and have fixed charges. Between 0630 and 2300 it is linked with Barcelona Central-Sants by a train every 20 minutes. Authorized taxis are relatively inexpensive (they charge supplements for the airport journey and for baggage). Do not take any other alleged 'taxis'.

Art de Catalunya, Museu de: This museum's collection of Romanesque and Gothic art is Catalunya's greatest artistic legacy. Displays are particularly well organized. Maps show the origins of works. Some exhibits relate the period's art to prevailing social conditions. There is also a fragmented collection of works dating from the 16th to 18thC. See MUSEUMS 1, **Romanesque**, **Gothic**.

Art Modern, Museu de: Collection concentrates on Catalan painters and sculptors. Strongest on first and second generation *modernista* and *noucentista* artists, with Casas, Rusiol, Sunyer well represented. The huge *Battle of Tetuan* by Fortuny is a star exhibit. Presently housed in an 18thC building shared with the Catalan Parliament, the museum is due to be moved to the Palau Nacional. See MUSEUMS 2.

Arts, Industries i Tradicions Populars, Museu de: Displays of ethnic material and traditional crafts from rural Catalunya and other parts of Spain.

Ayuntament: See BUILDINGS 1.

Babysitters: Not many hotels provide this service. Some may arrange for professional babysitters on request. Make enquiries in advance through your travel agent. You can also enquire locally about *guarderias*, creches.

Barça: During the Franco years, Barcelona's premier football club was a focus for expressing sentiment against the régime. Real Madrid, regarded as the government's club, was, and still is, its arch rival in the Spanish league. This rich club with over 100,000 members participates in many other sports and retains its high place in the popular consciousness of Barcelonans. Hearing the well-behaved supporters chant, 'Barça, Barça' and celebrating a home win is a memorable experience. See **Sports**.

Barceloneta: 'Little Barcelona', an l8thC urban renewal project constructed to replace the area taken by Philip V for the building of his Ciutadella citadel. A grid of working-class tenement blocks, many fish restaurants, a long beach and bathing facilities. See CITY DISTRICTS.

Barcino: Around 230 BC, the Carthaginians founded a settlement and named it after their great general Hamilcar Barca. Shortly afterwards it fell to the Romans whose emperor Augustus, around 13 BC, gave it the grand title of Iulia Augusta Paterna Faventia Barcino. It was built up as an administrative town within the imperial province of Tarraconensis whose capital was Tarraco (Tarragona). Archaeologists have uncovered a rich legacy of ruins and relics. Perimeter walls, of which parts remain, were built at the end of the 3rdC. As the Roman empire was collapsing in the late 4thC, Vandals and other raiding tribes appeared. Then the Visigoths, converts to Byzantine Christianity, took over as rulers of the peninsula and between 531-48 Barcino was their capital. Excavations below the cathedral are revealing evidence of this period. See **Moors.**

Barri Gòtic: The atmosphere-laden Gothic Quarter is one of the city's top attractions. It is so named because of its many well-preserved civic and domestic buildings from the 13th to 15thC. It was the site of the Roman city of Barcino and was within the protection of stout defensive walls. See CITY DISTRICTS, WALK 1.

Beaches: Barceloneta's are the nearest. Although the sand is relatively clean, the water is not. *Balnearios* (pools) in Barceloneta are an alternative. Best bet is to go to Castelldefels (20 km south). An even better plan is to go to Sitges (see EXCURSIONS). See also **Costa Daurada, Costa Maresme, Costa Brava**.

Born: In the barrio of Sant Pere-Ribera, Passeig del Born runs from Pl Santa Maria to Pl Comercial and the big iron structure of the Mercat del Born (by Josep Fontsere - 1876) now used as a venue for cultural events. Along the *passeig* are some lively bars and nightspots and off it, on the port side, some narrow streets with old-time shops and craft workshops.

Bourbons: The last Hapsburg king of Spain, who died childless in 1700, had nominated a Bourbon, Philip, Duke of Anjou as his successor. Another claimant to the throne, Archduke Charles, heir to the Holy Roman Empire, had most of Europe and parts of Spain, including Catalunya on his side. Thus Europe was thrown into the War of the Spanish Succession. After a 14-month siege Barcelona fell to Philip's forces in 1714. As Philip V he instituted the Nova Planta, a series of punitive measures against the Catalans and he built the Ciutadella fort to control them.

Bullfighting: Catalans have traditionally been less enthusiastic about this Spanish entertainment than the rest of Spain. Its aficionados regard the performance as an art form: a ritualized ballet in which the lurking danger to the man heightens the intensity. The fate of the toro is always the same. The Plaça de Toros Monumental has a limited season in the summer, there is also a small museum. Les Arenes bullring is mainly used for pop concerts. Probably the best idea for visitors who want to see the spectacle is to go with one of the tour operators. They provide a guide who gives an explanation of the performance and afterwards offers an assessment. (See **CITY TOURS**).

Buses: There is a good network for getting around the city cheaply and seeing it en route. Maps and *bonos* (saver tickets) are a help. Most of the routes pass around or near Pl de Catalunya. The regional bus station, Estacio del Nord, is at Av Vilanova, M Arc del Triomf. Services from this station run to Gerona, Costa Brava, Costa Daurada and also inter-city.

Call, El: The medieval Jewish quarter lay along the inner, east side of the city walls which followed the line of today's c/ Banys Nous and c/

de la Palla in the Casc Antic. Much of the area was destroyed in an anti-semitic rising of 1391 and in 1424 the Jews were expelled from it altogether.

Car Hire: All the big firms operate in Barcelona, either directly or with Spanish associates. Smaller, local firms whose leaflets may also be picked up at hotels and tourist offices usually have lower rates. Look out for special deals and term discounts. Compare all-inclusive costs as insurance and mileage charges often bump up the bill considerably. It's advisable to take comprehensive insurance which must include a bail bond. By law you should present a valid International Driver's Licence but usually your normal licence will suffice. See **Motoring**.

Catalan language: This distinct language, which written looks like an amalgam of Spanish and French but sounds more like Portuguese, began developing out of Provençal from the 7thC. It is now the native language of about seven million people, spoken with local variations in Catalunya, Valencia, the Balearic Islands, Andorra and the eastern French Pyrenees. Their language has been a strong unifying force for Catalans and its use was suppressed by Franco. Since the gaining of regional autonomy, Catalan has again flowered. Its teaching in places of education and use by local government bodies is now obligatory (see **Courtesies, Language**).

Catalunya: In 1979, this historically separate area or nation with its own language and many cultural differences, became one of Spain's 17 Autonomous Regions. It is divided into 38 *comarques* (districts) within the provinces of Barcelona, Gerona, Tarragona and Lleida. The Catalan Parliament administers the region through its executive body, the *Generalitat*. Catalans also elect members to Spain's Parliament, the Cortes, and the central government controls defence, foreign policy and, in the opinion of many Catalans, still too much of Catalunya's internal affairs.

Catalunya en Miniatura: Scale models of Catalunya's best known sights. A treat for kids. FGC train from Pl d'Espanya to Sant Vicenç dels

Horts, then walk (2 km) or take a taxi. Or off A2 at Exit 3.

Cathedral: La Seu. Begun in 1298 on the site of a Romanesque cathedral, most of the building was completed by 1450. The main (west) facade was only finished in 1892, following 15thC plans. Interior features are: its outstanding elevation, big bosses of the vault, the rose windows, carved and painted wooden stalls and marble screen of the *coro* (choir or chancel), the crypt chapel of Santa Eulalia who is co-patroness of the city, an elegant colonnade behind the high altar. Through the Porta de San Severo (a doorway from the Romanesque building) there's the cloister with its huge bays, chapels, gravestones in the floor, Gothic fountain, pavilion of Sant Jordi, green trees and a flock of noisy geese. Leading off here is the chapterhouse museum in which a *pieta* by Bermejo and a retable panel by Jaume Huguet (both 15thC) are the most notable exhibits.

Catholic Monarchs: Aragon, with which Catalunya was federated, and Castile were the two Christian kingdoms of Spain when Isabel and Ferdinand married in 1469. She became Isabel I of Castile in 1474 and he inherited the crown of Aragon five years later as Ferdinand II. Isabel had revived the Inquisition and they gained the title of Catholic Monarchs from the Pope for their zeal in spreading the faith. In 1492 they captured Granada, the last Moslem kingdom in the peninsula, and expelled all Spain's Jews who would not be baptised. Barcelona's economic and political power declined under their rule.

Cava: Sparkling wine made by the champagne method. Production is centred on the town of Sadurni d'Anoia in the Penedès region. The long second fermentation is done in huge underground cellars, some of which are open to visitors. Cordorniú and Freixenet are the leading brands and both have wide international success, outselling champagne in the United States. Quality and price vary quite a lot. Best quality is to be found among the drier Brut and Brut nature.

Ceràmic, Museu de: Attached to Museu d'Art de Catalunya. Anyone interested in ceramics should not miss this comprehensive display of wares, including beautiful, descriptive tiles, from Catalunya and other parts of Spain.

Children: They're made very welcome, almost anywhere and at any time. See CHILDREN for some enjoyable distractions. Also look in the local press for details of children's theatre, puppet shows and other events.

Cigarettes and tobacco: Smoking materials are sold in an *estanco (tabacos)*. Many have a selection of international brands. Spanish cigarettes are either *negro* (black tobacco) and strong like Ducados or *rubios* (blond) and mild like Fortuna. Well-made, strong or mild cigars from the Canaries are relatively inexpensive. Pipe tobaccos are mostly coarse and strong.

Cinema: Spain has an active and adventurous film industry. Most foreign films are dubbed. Showings in the original language with Spanish subtitles are advertised as 'v.o.'. The first showing is usually at 1630 and the last at 2230.

Civil War: The Spanish Civil War started when General Francisco Franco became leader of an army faction which, styling itself as 'Nationalist', rose against Spain's Popular Front Republican government in July 1936. From May 1937 to its fall in January 1939, Barcelona was home to the Republican government. The victorious Franco, installed as head of state, took severe revenge against Catalans and executed many Republican supporters. Expression of Catalan culture and the language were proscribed. Migration to Catalunya from the regions of Andalucia and Murcia was encouraged in the belief that it would weaken Catalanism.

Clara, Museu: Calatrava 27. 0930-1330 Tues-Sun. M Sàrria. Sculpture, drawings and paintings by Josep Clara (1878-1958), an acclaimed *noucentista*. Clara was a friend of Isadora Duncan (of whom he did many drawings) and for a long time was an influential figure in the city's art scene.

Climate: Typical of a Mediterranean climate, the rain falls in winter, mostly October-November and February-March when there can be long periods of cloudy weather. Average winter temperatures are mild (15 degrees centigrade) but the figure hides much colder snaps. In April-May the weather is less predictable, warm and sunny spells with sudden drenching downpours, followed by days of overcast skies. June and October are usually very pleasant months, ideal for less crowded sightseeing in comfortable weather. July, August and September are hot (averaging 28 degrees) with high humidity.

Collserola, Sierra de: The ridge of hills on the west of the city which helps moderate its climate, especially in winter, and of which Tibidabo (532 m) is the highest point.

Colom: In 1992, Barcelona, like the rest of Spain and much of the world, will celebrate the quincentenary of Christopher Columbus's first voyage to the Americas. It was to Barcelona that he returned in 1483 where he was received by the Catholic Monarchs of Spain, Ferdinand and Isabel, in the Saló de Tinell (Pl del Rei). Ironically, his discovery disadvantaged Barcelona. Europe's commercial interests gravitated towards the New World, diminishing Mediterranean trade and Barcelona was specifically excluded from the new trade which was centred on Sevilla and Cádiz.

Complaints: Places of accommodation, restaurants and petrol stations have to keep a *hoja de reclamación* (complaints forms in triplicate). If your complaint is about price, you must first pay the bill before requesting the forms. One copy is retained by you, another is sent to the tourism department of the regional government.

Consulates: Some 35 countries have consulates in Barcelona and more are likely to open before 1992. Most are located in the **Eixample**. For those not listed here, telephone directories give their addresses and numbers. Or ask your hall porter for help. *United Kingdom*, Diagonal 477, tel. 322 21 51; *USA*, Via Laietana 33, tel. 319 95 50; *Canada*, Via Augusta 125, tel. 209 06 34.

Conversion Charts:

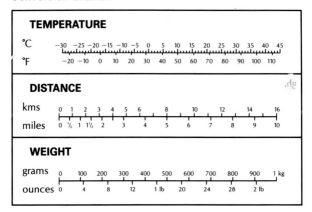

Costa Brava: North of Barcelona, the 'Wild Coast' of Gerona province where Europe's 'package' tourism began. Villages, small towns, residential developments and tourist complexes, some ugly, some tasteful, line a rocky coastline broken by small coves and sandy beaches backed by pinewoods. In the northern part there are dramatic cliffs, like on Cap de Creus; south towards Blanes, the shoreline is flatter. Development has spoiled the natural beauty in some places. In high season, the mass of foreign tourists overwhelm the native population but there are still many villages, resorts and secluded places in which to escape the crowds. Lloret de Mar is the largest, brashest resort. Tossa de Mar, which still has a charming old town, is getting that way. There is an impressive site of Greco-Roman remains at Empùries.

Costa Daurada: South of Barcelona, the 'Gold Coast' of Barcelona and Tarragona provinces, so named because of its many golden sand beaches. This coastline is getting increasing attention from the European package holiday industry but its impact is still limited, except in Salou and to a lesser extent in Sitges (see **EXCURSIONS**). Smaller resorts like Vilanova i la Geltrú and Cambrils retain most of their quieter ways and old charm. Castelldefels is the nearest resort to Barcelona and the city's people flock to its good beaches on summer days.

Costa Maresme: North of Barcelona and often included as part of the Costa Daurada, the 'Marsh Coast' extends from the city to meet the Costa Brava. It has good beaches and its resorts, like Canet de Mar, offer moderately priced accommodation, making them very popular with Spanish families. Arenys de Mar is a big sailing centre. Mataró and Premia de Mar are renowned for growing carnations, Spain's national flower. Much of the good quality fruit, vegetables and salads seen in Barcelona's markets comes from this fertile stretch of coastal plain.

Courtesies: Remember you are a guest in another country and the customs of your hosts are the norm here, not yours. Dress and behave with respect when visiting religious buildings. You'll notice that people don't like being rushed and don't care much for forming an orderly

queue. Catalans are generally quieter in public and more circumspect about expressing emotions than other Spaniards. Showing enthusiasm for their city is a good conversation starter and taking an interest in their culture and language will be appreciated. Two essential phrases: *si us plau* (please) and *gracies* (thank you). Going into a room, shop, elevator, or when formally meeting people, the greeting is *bon dia* (good day) or *bona tarda* (afternoon and evening). Leaving, it's *adeu* or *bona nit* (goodnight). A much-used phrase is *de res* (you're welcome).

Crime: Some advice: deposit your valuables in the hotel safe; carry the least possible amount of cash; take care about flashing money around and when leaving a bank; carry handbags and cameras on the off-street side; don't wear jewellery; walk with a friend or in a group; don't leave anything in sight in a car ; use taxis at night; be alert, and, importantly, show that you are. If you or a friend have been the subject of a crime, try to find witnesses and report the incident to the police immediately. Make sure to get a copy of your statement for insurance purposes. See CITY DISTRICTS, **Emergencies, Lost Property.**

Customs:

Duty Paid Into:	Cigarettes	or	Cigars	or	Tobacco	Spirits	Wine
E.E.C.	300		75		400 g	1.5 *l*	5 *l*
U.K.	300		75		400 g	1.5 *l*	5 *l*

Del Rei, Plaça de: Courtyard of the Counts of Barcelona's palace. Left from the entrance is the Palau de Lloctinent, l6thC with Renaissance elements, which contains the Crown of Aragon archives. To the right, the Casa Clariana/Padellas, (moved from elsewhere, stone by stone, to complete the plaça), houses the museum of city history. In the far right corner, a fan of stairs leads to a lobby from which there's access to the stark Santa Agata chapel with its impressive retable by Jaume Huguet (1465). Left from the lobby is the Saló del Tinell, a big and beautiful hall where Columbus was greeted by the **Catholic Monarchs** in 1493. Behind, rises the five-storeyed Mirador del Rei Martín a very early skyscraper (named after King Martin the Humane, 1396-1410). An enchanting place at any time, subtly floodlit some nights and a summer venue for open-air theatre. Extensive remains of Roman Barcino lie below the plaça and its buildings.

Dentists: see **Medical and Health.**

Diagonal, Avinguda: This wide avenue runs south west from Plaça de les Glories Catalanes (where it meets Gran Via) cutting diagonally through the **Eixample** and forming its top boundary in the central part. It leads to the A2 highway to Zaragoza and Madrid.

Disabled: Helpful facilities are still limited, toilets especially, although there is increasing provision by a socially aware city administration. Be sure to make full enquiries of travel agents or holiday operators before booking. Clearly state specific needs.

Domenech i Montaner, Luis: Born Barcelona 1850; qualified as architect, Madrid 1873; director of Barcelona's Escola d'Arquitectura 1901; died 1923. Leading Catalan nationalist politician, contributor to contemporary journals and historian of art and archaeology. He designed domestic and civic buildings and with the Palau de la Música he achieved the most outstanding synthesis of his style.

Drinks: Tap water is safe but heavily chlorinated. *Agua mineral, con gas* or *sin gas*, bottled mineral water, carbonated or uncarbonated. *Te*, tea is usually served with a slice of lemon. *Infusión de manzanilla* is camomile tea, very refreshing. *Horchata*, a cool, refreshing drink made from ground nuts. *Granizado*, iced, fresh fruit juice. *Café Solo* (black)

or *café con leche* (with milk). Chocolate, thick and creamy for breakfast or a nightcap. Various qualities of local and imported beer, *cerveza*, are available. *Una caña*, (about half a pint) draught lager, usually cheaper. *Sangría*, a mixture of varying potency - ice, soda water, red wine, brandy, fruit and juices. *Cava*, fine quality sparkling wine at good prices (see **Cava**). Sherry is called *Jerez* - *fino* pale dry, *amontillado* medium, *oloroso* heavier, sweeter. Brandies, *coñac*, vary from the rough to fine (10 year or older).

Drugs: Possession of drugs is illegal and bringing drugs into the country is subject to very harsh penalties. Drug policies were more liberal in the early 80s but attitudes have hardened to try and prevent the use of drugs, and the associated crime, becoming a problem.

Eating Places: The region's cuisine features in the current promotion of all things Catalan. It is often very good in even the humblest looking places. But for the most refined revival of traditional dishes go to one of the pricier restaurants where the new Catalan chefs are making their mark. All of Spain's regional cuisines can found in Barcelona. Basque cooking, based on sauces, generally has the highest reputation. There are an increasing number of foreign restaurants as well as franchise operations like McDonalds. There are a few vegetarian restaurants. Meal times: breakfast until 1100; lunch 1330-1630; dinner from 2100. Grading of restaurants, one to five forks, reflects the standard of the facilities rather than the cooking. In the topics **RESTAURANTS** the grading is as follows: a Budget meal will cost less than 1200 ptas for the main course, Moderate will cost less than 2000 ptas for a main course and Expensive more than 3000 ptas for the main course.

Eixample: *Ensanche* in Catalan, it means Extension. When in 1859 the engineer and planner, Ildefons Cerda, was commissioned to plan Barcelona's improvement and expansion, he proposed a grid of squared blocks intersected by two large diagonal avenues. Property developers commissioned the leading modernista architects. The part between the old city and the then village of Gracia saw the most elegant development and its two broad avenues, Rambla Catalunya and Passeig de Gracia,became, and still are, the show places for affluence and sophistication. High-priced real estate, commercial and residential, ensures the district's exclusivity. See **CITY DISTRICTS.**

Electricity: 220 or 225 volt. Round pin, two point plugs. Wiring colour-coded to international standard.

Emergencies: Dial 091 for the *Policia Nacional*. Concentrate on giving your location, nature of emergency and saying what other services may be required. *Ambulancias* 300 04 22. *Bomberos* (Fire Brigade) 080. Emergency Doctors 212 85 85.

Espanya Industrial, Parc de: An area, designed by Luís Pe a Ganchegui, featuring an artificial lake and several sculptures which, like the nearby Pl Països Catalans in front of Sants station, is an example of the city's *'urbanisme'* programme.

Fiestas: April 23 is the feast day of Catalunya's patron, Sant Jordi, and the Day of the Book and the Rose when people give each other a crimson bloom and a book. Sant Joan's day coincides with the summer solstice (June 23) and is celebrated with bonfires and fireworks. The Grec festival of theatre, music and dance starts in July and lasts for a month. Political events are a feature of Catalunya's national day, *Diada*, on September 11. In the week leading up to the feast day of Barcelona's patroness, *Merce*, there are galas and parades. The Christmas season starts off with the fair of Sant Llucia on December 13.

Flamenco: An explanation for the origins of flamenco is that after the Inquisition it evolved as the music of persecuted minorities who banded together in the mountains of Andalucia - gypsies of Indian stock, Moors and Jews. Four separate talents are expressed in a full performance: *cante* (singing), *baile* (dancing), *toque* (guitar playing) and *jaleo*

(rhythmic clapping and footwork). The best performers are said to have *duende*, an unquantifiable quality. *Flamenco jondo*, profound and melancholy, expresses the deepest emotions. Light and lively, *flamenco chico*, is more about sensuous love and sadnesses overcome. *Tablaos* at commercial venues usually present a mix of the two. See **NIGHTLIFE**.

Food: For breakfast there are *pastises*, croissants and brioches, or the heartier *esmorzar de forquilla*, which could be chops and vegetables. A favourite snack meal is *pa amb tomaquet*, bread spread with fresh tomato, seasoned with salt and olive oil, served plain or as the base for an open sandwich. *Sopas* (soups), like *escudella*, vegetables in meat stock, can be very filling. *Amanidas* (salads) too can often be a meal by themselves. *Pastes* (pastas) and *arròs* (rice) are both important in Catalan cuisine. *Peix* (fish) is fundamental to Catalan cuisine, just grilled, *a la planxa*, with a subtle sauce like the delectable *romesco* or in a dish like *sarsuela*, assorted fish boiled with tomatoes, peppers and peas. *Carn* (meat) is generally of a higher quality than in many parts of Spain and charcoal grilling is the preferred way of cooking it. The Catalans also make lots of tempting, light pastries and tarts.

Gaudí: Born Reus 1852; died 1926, after being run over by a tram.

Now the best-known architect of the *modernista* period, but then not part of the mainstream. Morally and politically very conservative and, in later years, consumed by his religous passion which he directed into the **Sagrada Família** cathedral. His work represented a separate tendency in which Jujol, Berenguer and Rubio became his main associates. He was at first inspired by historical styles and the use of traditional materials like red brick, ceramic tiles and ironwork. Later, more than any other architect, his forms follow the organic, flowing line of nature and appear more like sculpture. He carried his innovative ideas into the design of furniture, lighting and interior decoration.

Generalitat: see BUILDINGS 2.

Gothic: Architecture, in which the emphasis for creating space and grandeur is on the vertical rather than the horizontal, was brought to Catalunya by French Cistercians in the 12thC. In Catalunya, the trend towards verticality was less emphasized and a totally distinct church style with minimal decoration evolved. Cloisters have arcades of slender columns with decorative floral capitals and delicate tracery. These were also used in arcaded galleries built above the inner patios of mansions and civil buildings which, externally, are undecorated and solid-looking.
In painting, large retables with *esgrafiado* (embossed gold backgrounds) and *estofado* (raised gold haloes and clothing) remained the principal form. At the same time sculpture became much more delicate with naturalistic form.

Gràcia: Once a separate town with liberal and anarchistic traditions, it is now an inner city suburb which retains some of its small town atmosphere. Pl Rius i Taulet, its main square, has a 30 m tower decorated with signs of the zodiac.

Gràcia, Passeig de: Barcelona's most elegant boulevard, conceived in Cerda's 1859 plan, runs through the central part of the Eixample from Pl de Catalunya to Pl de Joan Carles I. See WALK 3, CITY DISTRICTS, MODERNISME, SHOPPING.

Gran Via de les Corts Catalanes: The city's widest avenue, conceived in Cerda's 1859 plan, runs south from Plaça de les Glories Catalanes (where it meets Avinguda Diagonal) cutting through the Eixample and forming its bottom boundary in the central part.

Guides: For personally tailored tours or business meetings, there are guides and interpreters for hire. Tourist offices have lists. During summer months, red-coated guides patrolling La Rambla and the Barri Gòtic will help with your queries.

Hairdressers: A *peluqueria* is where you go. They're plentiful and there's no shortage of places with good stylists. Many are unisex. Prices vary greatly from salon to salon so check before the stylist gets to work on your *pelo* (hair).

Hapsburgs: In 1520 the grandson of the **Catholic Monarchs** inherited a united Spain with its Mediterranean and American colonies. Four years later he inherited the title Charles V, Holy Roman Emperor, and the huge European domains of the Hapsburgs (Germany, Austria, the Low Countries and parts of France) from his paternal grandfather. In pursuit of their grand European designs and Catholic fervour against the Reformation, Charles and his son, Philip II (reigned 1556-1598), squandered Spain's wealth from the New World and exhausted the Spanish nation in endless wars. A Catalan vice-admiral and many men from the region helped Philip's brother, Don Juan of Austria, beat the Turkish fleet at Lepanto (1571). The smoke-stained crucifix from La Real, his flagship, is in Barcelona's cathedral, and a replica of the ship is in the Maritime Museum.

Història de la Ciutat, Museu de: There is an extensive subterranean display of remains from Roman Barcino. The bulk of its exhibits date from medieval times onwards. They show the importance of craft guilds, their associated religious brotherhoods and commerce in commissioning works of art. Plans and models show the development of the city. Especially interesting is the 1859 plan of Ildefons Cerda for the **Eixample** (Ensanche in Castilian).

History: See **Barcino, Moors, Counts and Kings, Catholic Monarchs, Hapsburgs, Bourbons, Civil War, Juan Carlos I.**

Hours: The Siesta, Spain's traditional afternoon rest, is under threat. Modern Spain cannot be asleep when its competitors are working. For many people, the journey from workplace to home takes too long to do it four times a day. More women are working and cannot be at home to prepare the large lunch (which induced the *siesta*). Factories and many businesses are now operating unbroken eight-hour shifts. Some government offices stick to the old times, others have changed. In summer, many places work one long shift, 0800-1500. So, it's all a bit confusing but here's a general indication: *Shops*: 0930-1330 and 1630-2000 Mon.-Fri., 0930-1400 Sat. *Department Stores*: 1000-2000 Mon.-Sat. *Business Offices*: 0900-1400 and 1630-1900 Mon.-Fri. *Government Offices*: 1100-1300 Mon.-Fri. (for business with the public). *Banks*: 0900-1400 Mon.-Fri., 0900-1300 Sat.

Juan Carlos I: The King of Spain was born in Rome in 1938, a grandson of Spain's last Bourbon monarch, Alfonso XIII. In 1962 he married Princess Sofia, daughter of the King of Greece. Franco had in 1969 named Juan Carlos to be his successor and when the dictator died in 1975 he was proclaimed King. Don Juan Carlos set a course steering the country to democracy under a new constitution (1978) which he has stoutly protected. With the Queen and their three children, Elena, Cristina and Felipe, he has created a popular and populist monarchy with little of the pomp and protocol surrounding Europe's other crowns. They use the Pedralbes Palace when visiting Barcelona.

Laietana, Via: Major thoroughfare cut through the Ciutat Vella in the city's *reforma* of this century's early years and named after the Laietani, the region's indigenous people.

Language: Castillian Spanish is Spain's official language. In Catalunya the Catalan language is given equal ranking with Castillian. All the people you are likely to meet will speak Castillian but some signs are in Catalan only. See **Catalan language**.

Laundries: Hotels have laundry and dry cleaning services. A *lavandería* (laundry) or *tintorería* (dry cleaner) is likely to be cheaper. They usually charge by weight and need a minimum of 24 hours.

Lost Property: If you have lost something tell the hall porter or a person in charge wherever you are staying. They may ring a central lost property office for you (tel. 301 39 23). If the loss is serious, report it to the Police (corner of Via Laietana/Comtal) and get a copy of your statement. Promptly advise credit card companies, issuers of travellers' cheques and, if your passport is lost, your Consulate. See **Police**.

Mail: The main Post Office (*Correos*) is on Plaça Antonio López and is open for general business 0900-1330 and 1700-1900 Mon.-Fri., 0900-1400 Sat. You may have your mail addressed here: Name, Lista de Correos, Pl Antonio López, Barcelona, Spain. Take your passport as identification for collections. Stamps (*sellos*) can also be bought from your hotel or tobacconists (*tabacos*). Mail boxes are yellow and red.

Manzana de la Discordia: The 'Block or Apple of Discord' (in Castilian *manzana* means both) on Passeig de Grácia has three

buildings demonstrating the styles of the principal *modernista* architects, Domenech, Puig and Gaudí. See **WALK 3** & **MODERNISME.**

Mare del Deu: 'Mother of God' is the title by which Catalans usually
refer to the Virgin. Unlike the rest of Spain, they have traditionally ven-
erated Mary more as a 'mother' than for her immaculate conception.

Media: Bookstalls at the upper end of La Rambla are open 24 hours,
except Sunday nights. *El País*, Spain's daily newspaper with the highest
international reputation, publishes a Barcelona edition. *El Periódico*, a
local daily in Castillian, gives good coverage to Barcelona. The conservative *La Vanguardia* espouses Catalan nationalism. *Cambio 16* is the
top weekly news magazine. *The Iberian Daily Sun* covers Spanish and
international news in English. Leading foreign newspapers and magazines are widely available, most European ones on their day of publication. There are both public and private radio stations, some providing
constant pop music. Overseas services of some other countries can be
picked up on medium wave at times or on short wave. TVE has two
television channels in Castillian. The third channel is Catalan. From
June to September Channel 2 features news in French, English and
German between 1230 and 1300. See **What's On.**

Medical and Health: It is foolhardy to travel without having a valid
travel insurance policy which provides substantial accident and health
cover. In Barcelona, your hotel or other place of accommodation, will
assist in calling a doctor or making an appointment with doctors or
dentists. Your consulate may provide a list of medical practiners. You
will be required to pay for each visit or consultation. Emergency cases
are usually accepted at both public and private clinics or hospitals.
Unless you have obtained an E111 (European Community Health form)
entitling you to treatment in EEC countries, you will be charged for
these services. On presentation of your insurance policy, practioners
and clinics may accept waiting for payment of bills from the insurers.
Farmacias (green cross sign) are chemist shops where prescriptions are
obtained. A notice on the door will give the address of the nearest on
duty chemist after normal hours. Obtain and keep all receipts.

Metro: Four metro lines and an urban rail link (FGC) from Pl Catalunya provide a fair, but not comprehensive, coverage. The system is clean and easy to use. Get a plan from any station. There is a cheap, flat fare and you can also buy 10-ride saver tickets.

Miró, Joan: Born Barcelona 1893; first one-man show 1918; lived in Paris 1920-1932 (but spent many summers at Montroig near Tarragona) and again during Civil War; moved to Mallorca 1940; died there 1983. He fused influences from abroad with what he saw naive, local artists doing and stated that his art reflected his Catalan experience. In the 1920s he gained international recognition as a leading surrealist. As a painter, designer, sculptor, ceramicist, who could brilliantly assemble colour, form, space and symbolism, he maintained a prominent position within the global artistic community until his death.

Modernisme: The dominant intellectual and artistic movement in Catalunya during two decades on either side of 1900. It modernized Catalan culture, opening it up to the world, while fortifying the sepa-

ratist tradition of Catalan society. Barcelona's Universal Exhibition of 1888 gave it a great, initial boost. *Modernista* architecture and its associated decorative arts provide the visitor to Barcelona with easy access to vivid characteristics of Catalan Modernisme. Like parallel trends elsewhere, Art Nouveau, Modern Style and Jugendstil, it was a rejection of cold, classical architecture to develop a rationalist style which could freely blend local traditions with new technology. Much of its inspiration came from Catalan Romanesque and Gothic and it also drew on *mudejar* styles. See **Domench, Gaudí, Puig**. Santiago Rusiol (1861-1931) and Ramón Casas were the leading *modernista* painters of the 1890s, with works which portrayed cafe scenes, street life and contemporary events. In 1897, together with the critic Miquel Utrillo, and the bohemian Pere Romeu, they opened the Els Quatre Gats tavern which became a lively venue for the promotion of *modernisme*. Hermen Anglada, Joaquim Mir and Isidre Nonell were the leading lights among the second generation of *modernista* painters.

Money: The peseta (ptas.) is Spain's monetary unit. Notes: 10,000; 5,000; 2,000; 1,000; 500; 200 and 100 (going out of circulation). Coins: 200; 100;50; 25; 10; 5; l. Banks offer the best exchange rate. Open 0900-1400 Mon.-Fri., 0900-1300 Sat. Essential to present your passport for any transaction. The major international credit and charge cards are widely accepted, as are travellers' cheques in any west European currency or US dollars and Eurocheques supported by a valid card.

Montcada, Carrer de: In the part of the Casc Antic which was the city's fashionable district from the 15th to 18th centuries, this narrow, evocative street runs from c/ de la Princesa to Santa Maria del Mar church. It is lined with fine residences from the period, notable for their plain exteriors, interior patios, stairways above an arch and some arcaded galleries. In the Lleó palace (no 12), used for the textile museum, there are elements from as early as the l4thC. The l8thC Aguilar and Castellet Palaces (nos 15-19) house the Picasso museum. An elegant staircase is a feature of the Dalmases palace (no 20). Art showrooms of Galeria Maeght occupy the Cervelló palace (no 25). Bars,

eating places and some interesting shops cater for the constant parade of sightseers.

Moors: The collective word describing Arab, Berber and other Moslems who invaded Spain from North Africa in 711 and rapidly gained control of the peninsula. But they did not stay long in this part of it. In 985 the adventurous Moorish general, al-Mansur, raided Barcelona, destroying the cathedral and much of the town.

Motoring: If you are coming to the city by car, the best advice is to park it in a secure place and use public transport, organised city tours and excursions.If you are taking your car to Spain, be sure to consult a motoring organization in your country and take out good insurance. If you hire a car and it breaks down, contact the company for instructions. Parking prohibitions are usually clearly marked by painted kerbstones and signs. Some petrol stations close on Sundays and holidays. You need the following with you when driving in Spain: passport, current driving licence (international or EEC), vehicle registration docu-

ment, third party insurance document and bail bond (usually covered by car hire agreement document), spare headlight, sidelight and rearlight bulbs, red warning triangle (if you're going on motorways). Minimum age is 18. Drive on the right. Overtake on the left. Give way to traffic coming from the right, especially at roundabouts, unless its clearly marked that your road has priority. Never cross a solid white line to overtake or turn left.

Speed limits are: 60 kph, most urban roads; 90 kph, other roads where indicated; 100 kph, main roads; 120 kph, motorways. Belts must be worn in front seats outside urban areas. Don't drink and drive (permitted maximum is 0.8 g alcohol per 1000 cc). Penalities for motoring offences can be severe and include prison terms.

Mudéjar: A Moslem under Christian rule. Also, the architectural style incorporating Moorish elements, mainly 13-16thC.

National Railway: Passeig de Gracia 13. M Plaça de Catalunya. This is the RENFE central office which provides information, reservations and tickets. The two main stations are linked: Central-Sants (M Sants) and Terme-Franca (M Barceloneta).

Nightlife: Its vibrant nightlife is one of Barcelona's big attractions. The best is to be found in the Eixample and beyond Avinguda Diagonal. A programme for a night on the town might be: start off at a *xampanyeria* or cocktail lounge, arrive at your chosen restaurant around ten. Then go to one of the fashionable music bars, a flamenco show, cabaret or dance hall. If you can keep going, move on to a disco. And end with a breakfast of anything you may care for at the Pinocho bar in La Boqueria market. You may prefer to spend the whole evening, including dinner, at one venue like Zeleste, Scala Barcelona or Patio Andaluz. Dress well, leave your tourist trappings behind and use taxis. See also **RESTAURANTS**.

Noucentisme: An artistic movement which followed *modernisme* in the first decades of the 1900s and was part of the general European trend towards classicism and realism. Paintings by Joaquim Sunyer and Feliu Elias and sculptures by Enric Casanovas and Josep Clara are examples of different styles within the trend.

Olympics 1992: The summer Olympics of 1992 are scheduled to start in Barcelona on 25 July, the feast day of St James (*Jaume*), Spain's patron saint. And *mes que mai* (more than ever) Barcelona will be presenting itself to the world. Some of the world's best-known architects are involved in the huge programme of building and urban improvement now underway. Of the 24 events in the Olympics, 19 will be held within a radius of five kilometres of the city centre. The Olympic Arena on Montjuic will be the main centre of activity. Stadia and swimming pools are being renovated and a new indoor sports centre, Palau Sant Jordi, has been designed by Arata Isozaki. Existing and new facilities in the Les Corts and Vall d'Hebron areas of the city, like F C Barcelona's stadia and the Velodrome respectively, will host other events. Competitors will be housed in the Olympic Village, designed by the famous Catalan architect, Oriol Bohigas, for a site between Parc Ciutadella and the sea.

Orientation: The city extends to some 20 sq km, bounded by the Mediterranean on the south east, the Sierra de Collserola hills on the north west, the Río Besos in the north and Río Llobregat in the south. It's 620 km from Madrid and 150 km along the A7 motorway from the Spanish/French border town of La Jonquera.

Palau Nacional: The monumental Palau Nacional was built as the centrepiece of Barcelona's International Exhibition of 1929. Reactionary in style at the time, it is of little architectural merit. See MUSEUMS 1, Art de Catalunya.

Passports, Visas: Tourists holding a valid passport of an EEC country or of the United States and Canada do not require a visa to enter Spain. Those with Australian, New Zealand, South African, Japanese and some other passports have to obtain a visa from a Spanish Consulate. Check with Travel Agent, Tour Operator or Spanish Consulate.

Pedralbes: An elegant residential suburb in the south western part of the city where some faculties of the university, the Palau Reial and Monastir de Pedralbes (see BUILDINGS) are located. At the lower end of Av de Pedralbes are a wrought iron gate and lodges designed by Gaudí for the estate of his patron, Count Güell.

Pedrera, La: The 'Stone Quarry', nickname given to Gaudí's Casa Mila. See MODERNISME 1.

Pets: Get details about taking pets from a Spanish consulate and check regulations for bringing the pets back. Few hotels welcome pets.

Photography: Film, development and printing is generally higher priced in Spain than in other countries. Rapid processing places give the standard quality service. Do not attempt to photograph policemen, military installations, planes or runways. Photography, or use of flash-light, is not allowed in some places of interest.

Picasso, Pablo Ruiz: Born Malaga 1881; arrived in Barcelona with his parents 1895; moved to France permanently 1904; returned to Catalunya 1906, 1909, 1910, 1917 and, briefly, a few more times until his last visit in 1934 before the Civil War; died, Mougins 1973. The young Andalucian was accepted into the *modernisme* milieu of Els Quatre Gats, illustrating its menu and having his first exhibition there. Nonell's images of society's outcasts, like his gypsies, influenced some of Picasso's Blue Period work, notably in 1902. In 1917 he designed the decor for Diaghilev's *Parade*, performed at the Liceu theatre, and returned to the city to enjoy his prestige. The Museu Picasso is based on a donation in 1960 by the artist's friend and secretary, Jaume Sabartes. In 1968 Picasso presented his *Las Meninas* series.

Police: The Policía Nacional are the tough, smart-looking men and women in khaki and brown uniforms and berets who walk the streets in twos and patrol in white or tan vehicles. Report any crime to them and make a formal statement at their *comisaría*. The Policía Municipal (blue uniforms, white or blue cars) deal mainly with the city's traffic and enforcing municipal regulations. You will see the Guardia Civil (green uniforms and tricorn hats) at immigration and customs posts and also patrolling roads and rural areas. Catalunya has its own police force (dark blue uniforms, red cap bands) which has a role somewhere in between the rest.

Public Holidays: Public Holidays are celebrated in Barcelona on the following days: 1 Jan., 6 Jan., 1 May, 24 Jun., 25 Jul., 15 Aug., 24 Aug., 12 Oct., 1 Nov., 8 Dec., 25 and 26 Dec. and on the variable feast days of Good Friday, Easter Monday and Corpus Christi.

Public Toilets: Some automated toilet cabins have been installed. An alternative is to choose a bar or cafe, use its facilities, then have something to drink there.

Public Transport: Plaça de Catalunya is the hub of the public transport network. The kiosk at the metro station below the plaça provides maps of the bus, metro and local train routes and sells *bonos*, saver ticket combinations.

Puig i Cadafalch, Josep: Born Mataró 1867; qualified as an architect 1891; president of the Catalan regional government (Mancomunitat) 1916-23; died 1957. Like his mentor, Domenech i Montaner, he was a leading Catalan nationalist politician and historian. Domenech and Gaudí were his strongest early influences then his inspiration became more cosmopolitan. After about 1915 he began to practise the modified classicism which became the vogue of Catalan architecture and he was involved in designs for the 1929 Exhibition.

Railways: The central RENFE office is at Passeig de Gracia 13 (M: Placa de Catalunya). You can get information, make reservations and book tickets here. The two main stations are linked: Central-Sants (M: Sants) and Terme-Franca (M: Barceloneta). Terme-Franca station has services from France and the Costa Brava. Services from Madrid, the Costa Daurada and most other parts of Spain link with Central-Sants station. Trains to the airport run from Sants. As there are different types of mainline trains and fare structures, it's wise to consult a travel agent or the RENFE central office. *Cercanías*, local trains, serve outlying sub-urbs and nearby towns.

Rambla, La: The singular of Las Ramblas -- de Canalete, dels Estudis, de Sant Josep, dels Caputxins, de Santa Mònica -- five connecting streets running from Pl de Catalunya to the port. Rambla is derived from the Arabic *ramla,* meaning torrent, and the torrent which once ran here was paved over in the 14thC. In the last century, plane trees were planted and ornamental streetlights, kiosks and flower stalls were installed. Enthralled visitors usually outnumber local people in the seemingly endless *paseo* by day and night along one of the world's most animated streets. The fun of street entertainers and the beauty of flower stalls contrast with the nastiness of street criminals and stalls where animals are kept in tiny cages. See **CITY DISTRICTS, WALK 2.**

Religious Services: Your Consulate will be able to provide current information on places of worship and times of services.

Renaixenca: The renaissance of Catalanism in culture, politics and

economic interests which began in the 1830s and of which the revival of the medieval poetry competition, Jocs Florals (1859), was a high point.

Romanesque: An artistic style, shared throughout Western Europe, which came to Catalunya earlier than the rest of Spain (c. 10thC). More than 2000 buildings (mostly churches) in the style survive. They are restrained and utilitarian with carvings on capitals and doorways. Square or octagonal church towers are prominent features. Boldly coloured frescoes and paintings on wooden panels adorned the churches' stark interiors. The style was in the Byzantine tradition and the purpose was to inform and instruct an illiterate populace. Wood carving too showed Byzantine influence -- rigid postures, clothes and hair arranged decoratively rather than realistically. In the early years of the 20thC Catalans became aware of their Romanesque heritage which was being lost in decaying churches. The *modernista* architect, Puig i Cadafalch, was prominent in studies which led to the saving of many of the art treasures now in the Museu d'Art de Catalunya.

Sagrada Família, Temple Expiatori de la: Gaudí took over the project in 1883 from Villar, who had intended it to be a conventional neo-Gothic church. He planned a grandiose and symbolic structure which was to have a tower of 170 m representing Christ, another for the Virgin, four dedicated to the Evangelists and 12 to the Apostles. And he clearly wanted to apply all his architectural knowledge and personal techniques, especially blending naturalistic and architectural forms. During his lifetime only the apse and four-spired *Façana del Naixement* (Nativity) were completed. Sculptures of animals, people and scenes are integrated into flowing forms like clouds, waves and sand dunes to relate biblical stories in stone. Gaudí left no detailed plans. Anarchists attacked the building in 1935 damaging Gaudí's scale model (subsequently reconstructed). Work which ceased during the Civil War was restarted in 1952 and the controversy about it has raged ever since. You enter the building site through the *Façana de la Pasió* (Passion). A lift in the other great facade takes you to a viewing platform for a dizzying view of the site and across the city. In the Crypt (almost completed by Villar) a small museum has plans and photographs of the project's progress. See MODERNISME 2, **Gaudí, Antoni.**

Santa Maria del Pi, Església de: Plaça del Pi, Barri Gòtic. M Liceu. Built 1320-1400, Catalan Gothic with single nave, large rose window and octagonal tower.

Sant Cugat del Valles: FCG from Pl Catalunya. Industrial, residential and university town, 13 km west of Barcelona, which grew around a Benedictine monastery founded in 878. The l2thC cloister is a Romanesque masterpiece. Art exhibitions are held here in summer. Thursday is market day.

Sant Pau, Hospital de: Av de Gaudí/Cartagena. M Hospital de Sant Pau. Hospital complex by Lluís Domenech on which his son Pere worked (1912-1930). Departments in a number of pavilions set in spacious gardens and connected by tunnels. Parts are open to visitors. Most notable is the entrance building with its strong *mudejar* elements.

Sant Sadurní d'Anoia: Small town 35 km south west of Barcelona

where the cellars of Cavas Cordorniú, by Puig i Cadafalch, can be visited on weekdays (closed August). Also 11thC chapel of Espiells and a
Roman bridge. Thursday is market day. See **Cava**.

Sants Just i Pastor, Església dels: Plaça Sant Just, Barri Gòtic.
M Jaume I. Built 1345-60 on the site of a church founded by
Charlemagne's son in 800. Good example of Catalan Gothic church
with single nave. Once the parish church of Aragon and Catalunya's
count-kings, it is today a favourite for fashionable weddings.

Sardana: Catalunya's national dance probably stems from a more
animated harvest dance of ancient times. On Sundays and high days,
dancers form a circle -- anyone and any number can usually join in --
link hands at shoulder height and with neat footwork go through an
intricate sequence of steps and pauses to the accompaniment of *la
cobla*, an eleven-piece band of wind instruments and a double bass.

Sàrria: An upper-class suburb adjoining Pedralbes. Many of the city's top schools are here and there are some very gracious homes in the lower folds of the Sierra de Collserola. See **CITY DISTRICTS**.

Sports: The city is home to F.C.Barcelona, founded in 1899. Camp Nou stadium has a capacity of 120,000 and another smaller football stadium which holds 16,000. There are visits to the museum, video show and the presidential box. 1000-1300, 1600-1800 Tues.-Fri.; 1000-1300 Sat., Sun., hols. M: Collblanc.
Other sports you can watch or play include *Pelota*, squash, golf and swimming. Local tourist offices can provide more information, including addresses of sports federations.

Tapas: Many bars in the city follow the Spanish, rather than Catalan, custom of serving *tapas* - appetizers, ranging from olives, nuts or crisps to small and tasty portions of meats, seafoods, omelettes, salads or vegetables. All are temptingly displayed on the counter so you can indicate what you want. Some are served hot. *Raciones* are larger portions.

Tapies, Antoni: Born Barcelona 1923; inauguration of Fundació Antoni Tapies 1987. Recently described in *Le Monde* as 'the most illustrious of contemporary Spanish painters'. He has exhibited very widely abroad and received many coveted awards. His tribute to Picasso (1983) is a fascinating fountain creation on the Passeig de Picasso.

Taxis: They are plentiful and inexpensive by international comparison. Black and yellow, they stand at ranks or can be hailed. They're free when showing a *libre* sign on the windscreen and a small green light on the roof. A list of supplements which may be added to the metered fare is shown in the cab.

Telephone, Telex, Fax: Hotels tend to add a big margin to the cost of communications services. Telephone: Cheap rate is from 2200-0800. Coin-operated booths require 5, 25 or 100 peseta coins. Place coins in sloping groove at top of coin box. Lift receiver, check for dial tone, then dial. Coins will drop into box as needed. Codes for Spanish provinces and other countries are given in the booths. For local calls dial the number only. For international calls, after tone, dial 07, wait for second tone, then dial country code plus area code (exclude initial 0) plus number. At Telefonica offices payment is easier and assistance is available. Telex and Fax at main Post Office (Pl Antonio Lopez) and from business services bureaux. Telegram: by telephone on 322 20 00 and at Post Offices.

Terrassa: FGC trains from Pl Catalunya. Catalunya's third largest city, 33 km west of Barcelona, developed as a major textile producer from medieval times. Its Museu Textil has an interesting collection of cloth and clothes from the area and around the world. Also interesting is the Cartuja de Vallparadis, a 13thC castle converted to a monastery in the 14thC, now restored and housing the municipal art museum. But absolutely fascinating, and worth a journey from afar, is the ensemble of three churches collectively called Les Esglésias de Sant Pere. Built in the 6-7thC and subsequently modified, they present a unique combination of Roman, Visigothic and Romanesque elements. In the Santa Maria basilica is a fresco depicting St Thomas à Becket's martyrdom and an impressive retable by Jaume Huguet, Catalan Gothic's master artist. Many modernista civic buildings, residences and factories can be seen in and around the city. Wednesday is market day.

Time Differences: Same time zone as Western Europe: one hour ahead of GMT and 6-12 hours later than the USA.

Tipping: Although it may not be shown separately, a service charge is included on all hotel and restaurant bills. But it's still the practice to leave around 5 to 10% in restaurants and to tip hotel staff for special services. At the bar, leave a token tip; 5 to 10% for table service. Taxi drivers, hairdressers and tour guides usually get around 10%. Lavatory attendants, doormen, shoeshines and car-parking attendants - 25, 50 or 100 ptas.

Tourist Information: Spanish National Tourist Offices in: Houston, London, Los Angeles, New York, Sydney and Toronto. The Municipal

Tourist Office is at Passeig de Gracia 35 (M: Paseig de Gracia) open 0900-1430, 1530-1730 Mon.,-Fri., 0900-1400 Sat. The Regional and National Office is at Gran Via Corts Catalanes 658, open 0900-1330, 1600-1900 Mon.,-Fri. The Municipal Office is inside a *modernista* building and has free leaflets and information. For cultural information contact the office of Cultural Activities at La Rambla 99 (M: Liceu).

Transport: The Plaça de Catalunya is the hub of the city's transport network. The kiosk at the metro station below the Plaça provides maps of bus, metro and local train networks and sells *bonos*, saver tickets.

Urbanisme: Barcelona's ambitious project of creating or remodelling squares, parks and gardens and endowing them with works by leading Spanish and foreign artists. Many of these improvements to the urban landscape have been undertaken in the city's working-class areas.

Villafranca del Penedès: 50 km south west of Barcelona. Main town of wine-growing area with interesting Museum of Wine (open Tues-Sat) and attractive old quarter. Market on Saturday. In the main square, a large monument to local *castellers*, the human pyramid builders for whom the town has a great reputation. Visits can be made to *bodegas* like Torres. Check at local tourist office. Market on Saturday. See **Sant Sadurní d'Anoia**.

What's On: Look for leaflets and posters at your hotel, tourist offices, cultural venues. Advertisements of events are posted around the city. *Guia del Ocio* is a weekly listings publication. The monthly *Vivir en Barcelona* is of a higher standard and more comprehensive. *El País* and *El Periódico* (see **Media**) have good listings, previews and reviews.

Wine: *Vino*, or *vi* in Catalan, is *tinto*, red; *blanco*, white; or *rosado*, rosé. Catalunya has five *denominaciones de origen*, officially demarcated and controlled wine-growing areas, of which Penedès, southwest of Barcelona, is the foremost. Its whites are fresh, fruity and aromatic, the reds smooth and light. The region's wines have a growing international reputation, due in large part to the ambitious Torres family proving that their high-tech *bodegas* can produce good quality wines in volume. Many restaurants will have a *vino de la casa*, house wine. Regional restaurants will feature both wines from their region in Catalunya or another part of Spain. Many will have a selection from Rioja, Spain's best-known wine region. See what local people are drinking or ask the waiter for advice.